CHILDREN IN THE LIBRARY

CHILDREN IN THE LIBRARY

A Study of Children's
Leisure-reading
Tastes and Habits

By

I. J. LENG

CARDIFF
UNIVERSITY OF WALES PRESS
1968

PRINTED BY J. D. LEWIS AND SONS LTD.
GOMERIAN PRESS : LLANDYSUL

To

Olwen, Val, Paul and Gareth

ACKNOWLEDGEMENTS

I WISH to thank the Librarian of the University of Birmingham for permission to refer to unpublished theses by M. Brearley, G. McDonald, M. Mullett and G. A. Philpott.

My boundless thanks are due to the Chief Librarian of *Llanfair* Public Library and those members of its staff who, day by day for an entire year, recorded the title of every book issued to each child using the Junior Library. Without the information thus collected, this work could never have been written.

It is a pleasure to acknowledge, too, my debt to the headmasters of the schools of *Llanfair*, who, on each of my many visits to their schools, showed me the greatest courtesy and afforded me every facility to carry out among their pupils the tests and enquiries needed for this study.

Lastly, to Professor D. W. T. Jenkins, whose unfailing encouragement and advice have made the task immeasurably lighter, I owe more than I can put in words.

CONTENTS

INTRODUCTION

A T each stage of progress towards universal literacy, at each extension of the means of disseminating ideas and information, at each new attempt to find a wider public for literature and the arts, there have been some to claim that our cultural standards are endangered. The first circulating libraries, the popular press, cinema, radio, television, even the early education acts, have all in turn been blamed for debasing public taste. The anxieties often expressed today need not perhaps be taken more seriously than previous premonitions of disaster, but no-one concerned with education can afford to leave out of account the many influences which affect, for good or ill, every effort to raise the level of our cultural life. In particular, the teacher whose purpose it is to improve the quality of children's reading is soon aware that the influence of the relatively few well-chosen books he may prevail upon his children to read at school is all too often out-weighed by the bulk of the reading matter they consume without prompting in their leisure time.

It is important, therefore, not only for the immediate purpose of school education, but also for the wider aim of raising the level of popular taste, to know how reading habits are first developed, what influences help to form our early reading tastes, what kinds of books children prefer to read at different stages, and what is the nature of the appeal they make. At the same time, it is not easy to lay aside our adult prejudices when considering the books which children voluntarily read. Judged by adult standards, few of them have any literary merit ; the majority are of an ephemeral kind, and even for their readers have only a transitory appeal. This alone is enough to arouse the suspicions of older people, especially of those whose literary training has disposed them to have regard for certain timeless and universal qualities in books. For children, these are not relevant considerations ; they can despise wholeheartedly today the very book they treasured a few months ago. Nevertheless, that book may have served its turn, and borne its reader one more step towards mature reading. We need to guard ourselves, therefore, against condemning the books enjoyed by children merely because they do not conform to certain prescribed canons. The task of the teacher, after all, is not to impose upon children certain books and to proscribe others, but to ensure that at each stage in their development the enjoyment they derive from reading is as full and deep as it possibly can be. We have to accept that the books which children will enjoy are those which speak to their condition, and that by and large they have an intuitive awareness of the kind of book which meets their needs. There is nothing to be gained in prevailing upon children to profess in school standards alien to those they apply in their leisure reading. They express their true tastes, not by protesting their regard for this or that classic, but in the quality of their daily reading.

This does not mean, of course, that the teacher can afford to temporize with the trivial and the worthless ; it means that he asks himself, not whether a book is good or bad in any absolute sense, but whether by reading it a given child is enabled to advance towards more mature reading. The teacher formulates his strategy, so to speak, in the light of his understanding of what is meant by literary merit and cultivated taste ; his tactics are determined by his knowledge of his pupils' capacities and needs. It is not a matter of insisting relentlessly on their reading at all times nothing but the best, but of bringing together the right book and the right child at the right time.

His main concern, that is to say, is that his children's reading be progressive, that each child should read books which challenge his growing powers of thought, feeling and imagination, and stimulate him to more ambitious sorties into the field of reading. We are familiar with the notion of progressive exercises in various branches of school work, including that of reading in the mechanical sense, but the idea of progressive reading for pleasure is less familiar, and perhaps less easy to accept. It is surely arguable, however, that we cannot afford to leave children without guidance in their leisure reading, an activity which plays so important a part in the shaping of their tastes, and thereby influences profoundly the quality of the cultural life of our society. And, if this is so, we need to understand how a child progresses in his leisure reading, by what gradations the reading tastes of the young child are finally transformed into the mature tastes of the full-grown human being.

The broad outlines of this metamorphosis are plain enough. In his passage from infancy to adulthood, the reader exchanges childish books, which deal in simple language and often under a guise of fantasy or allegory with a child's problems of adjustment to home, family and friends, for adult books dealing in more difficult language and in realistic terms with man's concern with the great problems of life, death, love, pain and immortality. As reading tastes mature, progress may be regarded as taking place on three different levels : in language, in themes, and in treatment. In the first place, as his reading skills improve, as he grows in the ability to grasp complex ideas, the reader chooses books of increasing difficulty, turning from simply written picture books to longer books employing relatively complicated language. Secondly, as he grows, his interests turn to increasingly adult themes, drawn from an ever-widening range of human experience, and involving progressively older characters. Finally, the element of fantasy so prominent in the books preferred in early childhood gives way to a much more realistic portrayal of character and situation : tales of toys and fairies are ultimately discarded in favour of stories about characters easily recognised as human.

What follows is in part an attempt to trace in detail the evolution of children's reading tastes in the course of their primary school lives. It is a record of the successive changes in language, themes and treatment that overtake the books which they prefer at different stages in their growth, such as will provide a yardstick, it is hoped, by which to judge whether a child's reading is keeping pace with his development, and to assess whether a given book is suited to a given reader.

More is required, however, than the mere record and description of the various books which children choose to read. Individuals vary widely in their preferences ; each child is unique in the combination of needs—intellectual, emotional and imaginative—which his reading seeks to satisfy. For this reason, it is not enough to know the books ; we need to know the reader also, the personal characteristics and environmental influences which have combined to make the story of his development as a reader different from that of every other child. The reader's mental calibre and educational level are obviously important factors : on them will depend the degree of language difficulty with which the child can cope in books ; it is likely, too, that the brighter and better educated the child, the more mature will be the themes and treatment which interest him. Sex differences cannot be ignored : they will be reflected, one expects, not so much in language as in themes and treatment. The part played by the home in forming reading tastes, while plainly of the greatest importance, is more difficult to assess. The nature of its influence is probably related to some extent to educational level and the economic status of the parents, and may be roughly gauged from the father's occupation. The son of an unskilled worker, one might guess, is likely to admire different heroes from those who would appeal to the son of a professional man, and in other ways to reflect in his reading the different ideals and values he has acquired from his experience. Another aspect of the reader's home environment can be expected to influence his taste in books : the nature of the personal relationships he enjoys within the family are vital to his entire emotional development and therefore, at least indirectly, to the nature of the demands he makes on books. It is likely, for example, that the child who has brothers and sisters will have not only less time for reading, but less need for the companionship of books.

Pursuing these hypotheses, we shall try to assess the effects upon the growth of reading tastes of sex, mental ability, educational attainment, parental occupation and family circumstances. This involves comparing, in respect of language, themes and treatment, the books enjoyed by contrasting groups of children. To give one instance, books read by boys and girls of high educational achievement are compared with those read by children of relatively low attainment, in an effort to determine the degree to which maturity in reading tastes is related to school performance.

Children's tastes are reflected in the nature of their choices, in the quality of the books they read ; their habits, on the other hand, are manifested in the quantity. And the same factors which determine tastes play a part in the formation of reading habits. A great deal of effort on the part of teachers goes into the task of inculcating reading skills ; fully as important is the task of nurturing the disposition to make regular use of them, the task, that is, of fostering the reading habit. Yet the Crowther Report provides an alarming indication of the extent to which our efforts in this direction fall short of success, especially among the boys who leave our secondary modern schools.[1] It is of more than academic interest therefore to understand exactly how the reading habit is acquired, who they are who resist it, and what conditions help its growth. Individuals vary as widely in the volume of their reading as in the quality, and it is the further aim of this enquiry to record these variations and, if possible, to explain them.

---

[1]Central Advisory Council for Education—England : *Fifteen to Eighteen*, Vol. II, p. 98. H.M.S.O. 1959.

The account which follows is based upon an examination of the books which children borrow from the public library. The one selected, *Llanfair* Public Library, serves a population of slightly less than 17,000 people, of whom 34 per cent make use of it to borrow books. It has a highly attractive Junior Department which some children join even before the age of three, and which others continue to use beyond the age of thirteen at which they can be admitted to the Adult section. They are entitled to take out one book daily, making their choice from more than four thousand books displayed on the shelves and some thousands more available upon request. Obviously, then, this is the richest source of books available to the children of the area, but at the same time it is not the only source, nor perhaps the most accessible. Some children will rely solely upon books found at home or school, lent by friends or received as gifts. For many, such sources will in any case be meagre and, at least for the more avid readers among them, quite inadequate. Even so, there will be children, avid readers among them, who never visit the library, but who find books sufficient for their needs elsewhere, while even the most assiduous users of the Public Library almost certainly read other books as well. So far as individuals are concerned, it would be a mistake to assume that because one child does not visit the library, he or she is not interested in reading, or that because another borrows more books, he or she is necessarily the greater reader. Nevertheless, in general the use made of the children's library may fairly be taken as an indication of the degree of interest children show in reading, and, even more accurately, as a reflection of their tastes in books.

The frequency with which a child will visit the Public Library depends to some extent upon its nearness. *Llanfair* Public Library is centrally situated in the town, but to minimise the effects of distance the investigation was confined to those children who were resident within a radius of one mile of the Library and who also attended one of the five primary and two secondary schools in the same area. It was limited also to children who, on May 1st, were more than six and less than thirteen years of age, a total of 1,055 children.

Over a period of one year, from September 1st to August 31st, a careful record was kept at the Public Library of every book borrowed by each of these children, each title being entered in the member's record as it was issued. Every effort was made to ensure that the record included only those books which had in fact been read by the child. On returning a book to the Library, the borrower was asked if it had been read and how much it was enjoyed. The possibility remained of a member's ticket being used by another child. Once in each term, therefore, each member was asked to check the list of books issued in his or her name in the previous weeks, and to indicate those which he or she had not read.

Of the 1,055 children within the scope of the enquiry, 555 made use of the Library in the course of the year. Part of our purpose was to discover how these were distributed by age and sex, to find what proportion of boys and girls of different ages borrowed from the Library, and to what extent, and thus to chart the growth in prevalence and intensity of the reading habit among children from year to year of their primary school lives.

Between them, they borrowed in the year about eleven thousand books. A list of the titles, apart from being unwieldy, would be uninformative to most adults, since the majority of them proved to be recent publications, intended strictly for children, and for the most part enjoying only a fleeting popularity. While fashions in authors and in titles change fairly rapidly, however, the basic themes which interest children are less mutable. In order to convey a picture of the way in which children's tastes change and develop as they grow, an attempt was made to classify according to their content the books which children borrowed at each age.

Any such attempt to classify books is inevitably crude. Even the distinction between fiction and non-fiction is far from clear-cut in many cases, while between Historical stories and Adventure stories, School stories and Mystery stories, Family stories and Careers novels, there are large numbers which might just as easily be ranked on one side as the other. For that reason, an attempt has been made to analyse more closely the content of these books, to record the kind of setting in which the story is located, the age and sex of the main protagonists, and the type of activity in which they are engaged, in the expectation that these will vary consistently according to the age and sex of the readers.

Moreover, it seems clear, the books which children choose as they grow older will tend to become more difficult. In order to verify and illustrate this, note has been taken of the format, the number of pages, the proportion of illustration, the size of type and the difficulty of language of every book issued, with the exception of those borrowed only once, and on each of these counts the norm or average calculated for readers of each age-group. These external aspects of the book are clearly important to the child, and play a great part in determining his choice, since he must inevitably be deterred if a book, however attractive its title or apparent theme, appears too big, has too many pages, too few pictures, too small a print and too difficult a style for him to enjoy.

Fortunately it is a fairly easy matter to count pages and pictures, measure format and print, and assess the difficulty of language. For these there are objective standards of a kind which do not exist for measuring the degree of realism of a book. Yet, we believe, one essential change that takes place in children's reading tastes as they grow is the gradual abandonment of make-believe and the progressive acceptance of a greater degree of realism in the books they read. This reflects itself chiefly in the portrayal of characters. Whereas toys, puppets and fairies predominate in those chosen by the very young, human beings endowed with ordinary human qualities people the books enjoyed by adults. In the intervening years, readers pass through the stage of preferring stories about characters who in external appearance are completely human but who possess attributes or engage in activities not ordinarily found in real life. If to the first stage we may apply the term Fantasy, and to the last that of Realism, this intermediate stage we may call that of Romance.

Each of the books issued to these children has therefore been classified according to the nature of its characters as Fantasy, Romance or Realism, and calculations have been made of the proportions of each among the books issued to readers at different ages. Laborious though the process may appear, it is one which enables us to approach what is perhaps the most fascinating question of all those which can be raised about children's reading : What is the relationship between the imaginary experiences they derive from books and the real experiences of life? And this, in turn, leads to the further question of why it is they read at all.

In order to shed light upon this second question, an attempt has been made to find out in what ways children who make use of the Library differ from those who do not. This aspect of the enquiry entailed the investigation of the intelligence, academic background, the social and family circumstances of readers and non-readers. This proved more than could be done for every child in the area, and it was decided that only those who were in their last year in the primary or the first year in the secondary schools would be considered. For each of these children, more than three hundred in number, information was collected by means of tests and questionnaires as to educational attainment, intelligence, parent's occupation and size of family. The relationship between each of these factors and children's reading habits and tastes was considered in turn. Children of high intelligence have been compared with those of low intelligence, in order to discover whether the former are more prone than the latter to make use of the Public Library, and whether the books they generally borrow tend to differ significantly in language, themes and treatment. In the same way, the academically able have been compared with the weaker scholars, those from manual with those from non-manual workers' homes, those from large with those from small families.

Membership of the Library is freely available to all ; all the books in it are equally accessible to every child. If, therefore, children differ from one another in the extent to which they use the Library, and in the nature of the books they borrow, these differences may fairly be said to reflect different attitudes to reading. This is not true of all their reading ; the books, newspapers and periodicals each child can read at home will differ from those available to every other child. It would be a mistake to compare the reading habits of different children unless all had equal opportunity to read. Too often, after reading accounts of investigations into children's reading, one is left with the uneasy feeling that one has learnt more about the reading matter they find available than about the kinds of books they are genuinely looking for. In the present study, the focus of attention is upon the child himself in the act of choosing for himself a book to read. The outcome, it is hoped, will be a clearer understanding of the factors which affect his choice, of the motives, conscious and unconscious, for which he reads, and of the bearing which his reading has upon his mental, emotional and imaginative life.

CHAPTER I

THE GROWTH OF THE READING HABIT

W E cannot but be aware of the extent to which the habit of reading pervades our lives today. It is a phenomenon we accept as natural, without surprise and even with cynicism. Yet to read, to derive meaning from graphic symbols, demands a complicated skill which does not come by instinct. Today, the average person by the age of twelve has of that skill enough to read with ease and pleasure, but for the majority of our people that skill has been within their reach only since the revolution in education in the last century. In the comparatively brief time that has since elapsed, the habit of reading has so spread that few indeed are untouched by it.

The Society of Young Publishers, in a small-scale survey carried out in London in 1959, found that 59 per cent of those they questioned were then in train of reading a book ; 17 per cent only had not read a book within the previous month.[1] Similarly, among adolescents the Westhill survey[2] found that all but a small proportion, again 17 per cent or so, were well used to reading books. And among school-children, Jenkinson (1940) found that an even smaller number, perhaps five or six per cent, seemed not to read books in their leisure hours. There are some who can never read. By reason of mental disability or other handicap, perhaps ten or fifteen per cent of the people of this country fail to acquire that level of skill which is necessary for adult reading. Remembering this, we are forced to recognise that virtually all in Britain who can read have to some degree contracted the habit of reading, whether it be of newspapers, periodicals, or books.

To take books alone, the number of titles published annually in Britain has in recent years exceeded twenty thousand. Public libraries play a vital part in their dissemination. Of the people interviewed in London, 34 per cent had borrowed the last book they read from a library, while 54 per cent had borrowed from a library at some time or another. In Llanfair, 34 per cent was again the proportion of the

---

[1] *The Bookseller.* Jan. 16, 1960. Pp. 122—124.
[2] Westhill Training College, 1950.

population found to be registered borrowers from the Public Library, and these took out an average of about forty books in the year, while for the country as a whole the statistics published annually in the Library Association Record testify to the use made of our public libraries by the adult population.

The question that arises is how the habit grows. At what age is it acquired, and once acquired does it persist ? There is good reason to believe that the thirty per cent or so of the population who continue to borrow from our public libraries in adult life form only a small proportion of those who have at some time in their lives been in the habit of doing so. The Crowther Report points out that of the boys who receive their education in our grammar schools, 89 per cent are members of a library at some period while they are at school, but within two years of leaving school the proportion falls to 55 per cent. An even steeper decrease occurs among boys from secondary modern schools, from 68 to 16 per cent.[1] A study of eleven thousand children over eight years of age, carried out by East Ham Public Libraries in 1934, found that 68 per cent of them were members of a library, 45 per cent of them being considered active members. Among children aged from seven to eleven, Brearley (1949) found 34 per cent of them to be library members, while Mullett (1951) found that among grammar school boys aged eleven to fourteen years, 36 out of 70 (51 per cent) used the public library. He cites other evidence indicating that at about this period in their lives, a fairly sharp decline occurs in the use boys make of the public library. All this suggests that library membership, gradually increasing throughout childhood, reaches its peak at some point during early adolescence and thereafter undergoes a decline until among adults it is confined to the thirty per cent or so who form the hard core of committed library readers. If this is the case, the library habit follows much the same pattern of development as has been traced in the growth of leisure reading habits in general. Terman and Lima (1931), for example, state that interest in reading approaches a climax of intensity at the age of twelve and afterwards declines in the years of high school education,[2] though neither Jenkin-

---

[1]Central Advisory Council for Education: "15 to 18", Vol. II, p. 98. H.M.S.O. 1959.
[2]Terman and Lima : 1931. p. 38.

son (1947) nor Scott (1947) finds evidence of any great loss of interest in reading before the age of fifteen.

From the evidence of the library reading of the children of Llanfair, it seems that Terman and Lima are probably correct in locating the peak in later childhood or early adolescence. Indeed, if we were to consider only the numbers of children who join the library, we should conclude that among the twelve-year-olds the popularity of the library is already on the wane. On the other hand, the average number of books taken out by readers is highest among the twelve-year-olds. We need to consider separately, therefore, the membership and the rate of borrowing as two somewhat contradictory indices of the popularity of reading among children.

Library Membership, Boys and Girls

Defining a member as a child who took out from the Library at least one book in the course of the year, we find that of the 1,055 children within the purview of the enquiry, 555 (53%) became members during the year.[1] The proportion of each age-group who joined rose steadily from 30 per cent of the six-year-olds to 67 per cent at the age of ten, thereafter falling to 61 per cent at eleven, and to 56 per cent at the age of twelve.

There are a number of explanations for this curve. The very youngest members were found to visit the Library in the charge of adults, the slightly older ones in the company of bigger children, brothers, sisters, or friends. In their early years, therefore, children are dependent on the good will of their elders for the opportunity to borrow books. There may well be some who, despite their interest in reading, fail to find an older person willing to accompany them to the library, and for that reason the figures of library membership may not give a very faithful indication of the extent of interest in reading among the very young. Older primary school children, however, usually appear at the Library with groups of companions of their own age. For them the visit is a social occasion ; they acquire from one another the habit of attending the Library and, to a large extent, their tastes in books. The important point is, however, that at this age visiting the Library is a group activity which no doubt attracts a number whose interest in reading is not in itself enough to take them

[1] See Appendix, Table 1.

there alone, or who would not be able to attend if they were obliged to rely upon their elders for company to go. Among those who join the Library at this period of their lives, there are undoubtedly some whose main interest is not in books but in the companionship of others, and who will in later years abandon the reading of library books for other activities which continue to offer opportunities of mixing with others. Those who continue to patronise the Library at the age ot eleven or twelve tend to go alone or with a single friend to borrow books. In all probability it is these who become the dedicated readers, whose interest in books is strong enough for them to forgo the companionship ot others for the solitary joys of reading.

There are other reasons for the steady increase in attendance at the Public Library in the years of primary school life. It is to be expected that as with growth more and more children acquire the ability to read, more and more will seek opportunities to exercise their skill and to reap its benefits. Membership of the Library rises most steeply between the ages ot nine and ten, when the rudimentary reading skills have been mastered by the great majority. Unquestionably, one of the satisfactions which children derive from reading is that which comes from the exercise of their skill. We have often seen children, having learned, let us say, to skip, thereafter skipping endlessly, repetitively, and apparently with no other purpose than to skip. This pleasure in an activity for its own sake is also part of the attraction reading has for children. The content of the book, the interest of the subject-matter, are often of only secondary importance ; children will often read with evident enjoyment what is apparently quite unsuitable material, simply to develop or display their virtuosity as readers. The point will emerge more clearly when we come to consider the vocabulary and sentence structure of the books these children customarily read, but it is worth saying here that the sense of achievement which a child derives from having read a book to the very end is no small part of the total satisfaction he experiences in reading. In any reading programme intended for young children it is important therefore that there be an adequate provision of simple books which the reader can complete almost effortlessly.

Even in the early stages, of course, children read for other purposes than the exercise of their skill. They very soon become aware that their achievement in school work hinges to a large degree upon their reading. This may in part account for the fact that so many of these children join the Library in their last year in primary schools before examination for selection for secondary education. It is certainly the case that after this point a number of them lose interest in the Library, and it is probably true of some of these that they read not so much for pleasure as in the hope that it will bring success at school. There is reason to believe, as will appear, that such children rarely become devoted readers.

It is not to be taken that children generally read for such conscious and utilitarian purposes. Rarely are they able to give any reason for reading other than that they enjoy it ; they are largely unaware of the basic needs they seek to satisfy through books. But in a sense, the pleasure which they feel is incidental, an overt sign of the fact that such needs are being met. And it is because these needs are most urgent in the period of development prior to adolescence that interest in reading is most widespread at this stage and afterwards begins to wane.

Apart from his physical needs, perhaps the deepest need to which the growing child is subject is for experience, for opportunities to realise his full potential as a human being. He is prey to curiosity about the world of things and people outside himself ; he is dimly aware of capacities within himself for feeling, thought and action, which demand outlet and expression. These are part of the primal urge to grow, change and develop, which constantly impels him to seek out new experiences, to push against the boundaries of the world with which he is familiar in order to give himself more elbow-room. This ceaseless effort to extend his field of action may be observed even in the very young. No sooner is the infant fully accustomed to the safety of his mother's arms than the growing power of his muscles prompts him to kick free of her embrace and make trial of his legs on the kitchen floor. From the kitchen he ventures to the garden, from the garden into the street, each fresh field offering new sensations, demanding new adjustments and evoking new skills, until finally it is out-grown. In exploring the external world, he discovers himself ; each new experience evokes from him a new response, and he grows not only in understanding of the outside world, but in awareness of the resources of his own nature.

Reading ministers to the child's need for ever wider, deeper and more varied experience. The more restricted the reader feels his opportunities for real experiences to be, the more urgent is his need for the vicarious experience offered him in books. Until the age of ten, as they grow older, more and more of these children have time and energy to spare for reading library books. Evidently the activities which have hitherto occupied them are no longer capable of absorbing their whole interest and attention ; visits to the Library and the reading of library books appear to increasing numbers of children interesting ways of passing time. It is not simply that they have more time to spare for reading however ; behind their desire for new ways of spending their leisure, one may sense their impatience with the restrictions imposed on them in every-day life, with the obstacles and prohibitions which hinder their search for novel experiences. Reading enables them to overcome these barriers, to be anyone, to go anywhere and do anything they please. Ten-year-olds especially appear to chafe against the restrictions of their day-to-day existence, and to need the opportunity reading affords for the imaginative exercise of their growing physical, emotional and intellectual powers.

Fewer eleven-year-olds borrow from the Library. For some of them, no doubt, once the selection examination is over, the main reason for reading library books no longer exists, while for others the fresh calls made on them now that they are in secondary schools leave them little time for reading. The new subjects they now meet, and the homework they are now expected to do, bring new interests into their lives and leave them not only with less time but with less need for library books. At the same time, with the ending of their primary school lives, many of them gain a greater measure of freedom than they have hitherto enjoyed ; they move in a new environment, meet new people and engage in new pursuits, in all ways leading lives fuller and more varied than before. In these circumstances, fewer of them feel the need for the substitute experience afforded them by books.

Fewer still of the twelve-year-olds make use of the Library.[1] Most children by this time are fluent readers, and the urge to practise and improve their skill is on the wane ; the selection examination, which was an additional incentive to reading, is now past ; the larger world of the secondary school pupil and the adolescent is now open to all. In later years, no doubt, they will again come to think their lives

---

[1]Between the ages of 10 and 12 years, the decline is statistically significant. Chi Square 4.38 ; P <.05.

irksomely restricted, and again turn to reading in order to widen their horizons, but in all likelihood the numbers using the Library continue to decline for some time beyond the age of twelve, since at 56 per cent the proportion of members among the twelve-year-olds is still far higher than among adults.

Volume of Borrowing, Boys and Girls

Though membership of the Library declines after the age of ten, there is no decrease in the number of books borrowed by those who remain members. On the contrary, the average rate of borrowing rises continuously from 14.5 books per member at the age of six to 26.5 per member at the age of twelve.[1] We have no means of knowing whether this increase continues, but it perhaps is relevant that the average issue to adult members of the Library is approximately forty books a year. What seems to happen between the age of ten or so and adulthood is that many of those who have used the Library cease to do so, while those who retain their membership increase their amount of reading. A winnowing process seems to take place, in which the less enthusiastic readers gradually fall away, leaving finally only a relatively small core of inveterate readers, comprising perhaps a third of the adult population.

That this is in fact what happens between the end of childhood and maturity is entirely conjectural. It is supported, however, by the fact that at some time in the intervening period a decline takes place in the numbers making use of the Library, accompanied by a steep rise in the rate of borrowing of those who do so. Moreover, there is evidence that this is already happening between the ages of ten and twelve. A comparison of Figures 1 and 2 shows that in this period membership of the Library declines while the rate of borrowing continues to rise. Prior to this the steady rise in membership from year to year is accompanied by a similar rise in the rate of borrowing. It is to be expected that, as in the years of their primary school lives their reading skills improve, children will read more. A number of investigations have shown that a positive correlation exists between reading achievement and the number of books read.[2] This is only to be expected,

---

[1] See Appendix, Table 2.
[2] The correlations reported appear to range from +0.30 (Lipscomb, 1931, p. 61) to +0.44 (Wollner, 1949, p. 78).

Figure 1

LIBRARY MEMBERSHIP AT EACH AGE
Boys and Girls combined

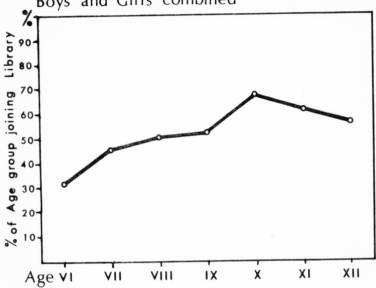

since the habit of reading brings about an improvement of reading ability, and that improvement in turn makes possible more rapid and extensive reading. The correlation, however, is not perfect; the number of books a child may read does not depend entirely upon the level of his reading ability. A child of very low reading ability may nevertheless read large numbers of simple picture-books which demand virtually no reading skill. In such a case reading ability would be expected to correlate more closely with the length and difficulty of the books selected than with their number.

Even so, the steady rise in the average rate of borrowing on the part of Library members which goes on during the years of primary education is no doubt largely due to the improvement in these years of their ability to read. In all probability also, it is the weaker readers who beyond the age of ten begin to fall away, in many cases perhaps because their reading skill has not progressed sufficiently to enable them to read the kind of books which are of interest to them at this age. The continuing rise in the average rate of borrowing on the

Figure 2
RATE OF BORROWING AT EACH AGE
Boys and Girls combined

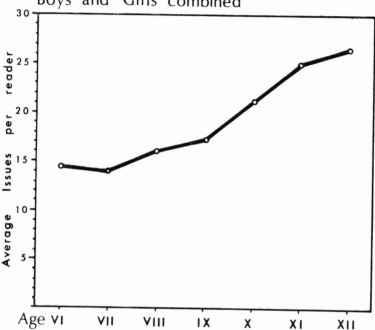

part of surviving members is mainly due, no doubt, to their higher average ability, but other factors are probably involved. Even the weakest readers are not entirely debarred from using the Library. Their choices may be restricted to the simpler books, but these exist in adequate numbers and in fair variety. Children of low ability can, and, though in diminishing numbers, do, make considerable use of the Library even beyond the age of ten or eleven, while others of higher ability fall away. The decisive factor in such cases is not the level of reading ability but the degree of interest in books. The two are obviously related but by no means inseparable.

At the age of ten more children are attracted to the Library and more books are borrowed on an average than at any previous age. Among those drawn to the Library at this time, however, there are many whose appetite for books, keen though in some cases it may be, fails to survive the following year or two. Many youngsters at about this time appear to experience a short-lived and superficial interest in reading, less perhaps as a means of exploring new spheres of thought and feeling, less as a means of real growth than as an expedient for relieving boredom, and especially that boredom to which restrictions on their physical freedom give rise. Many, that is to say, join the Library at about the age of ten for want of anything better to do, and of these the majority discontinue their membership as soon as other pursuits become available. The new interests and activities which become possible to boys and girls on leaving the primary school inevitably distract a number of them from their reading. Among those who resist these fresh attractions and who maintain their membership of the Library beyond the age of ten or eleven will be those for whom reading meets deep-seated and enduring needs.

There are two phases, therefore, in the propagation of the reading habit among children. The first extends from infancy until about the age of ten, a period in which the majority of children at some time or other give reading a trial, and many of them use the Library to do so. There follows a period in which some turn increasingly to other activities which they find more satisfying, while others develop a growing appetite for books. The child's final attitude to reading is largely shaped in the years immediately following his tenth. This is not to say that an enduring taste for books may not be implanted at an earlier age, but simply that it is impossible to predict whether even the most voracious reader in childhood will continue to read in adolescence. The eleventh and twelfth years are momentous ones in the life of every child. New and difficult adjustments are called for to unfamiliar schools, to fresh privileges and responsibilities, to un-suspected needs and impulses within themselves. However profitable or satisfying reading may have appeared to the child in earlier years, it will not seem to serve any useful purpose in the present unless he manages to find books which are in some way relevant to the complex personal adjustments which he has to make. An essential task of the teacher at this stage is to help the individual to find such books. The foundations of an abiding interest in reading are laid if, at the time when the individual is seeking new, more mature and more satisfying modes of thinking, feeling and acting, books make an effective contribution to the search.

Boys and Girls compared

Nothing can be done, however, unless the child is prepared to give reading a trial. Though in this country every child is given at school some opportunity to become acquainted with books, not all children have the same facilities, encouragement or disposition to give their leisure-time to reading. It is widely held that boys differ from girls in their attitude to books. Many studies carried out in various parts of Britain, in New Zealand and the United States among subjects of different ages lend support to the conclusion reached by Lehman and Witty (1928) that at every age from eight and a half to twenty-two girls express more interest in reading than do boys. The bulk of the evidence goes to show, moreover, that girls surpass boys in the amount of leisure-reading that they actually do. Opinion is not quite unanimous on this point, however. Lehman and Witty themselves consider that though boys express less favourable attitudes to reading, they do not in fact read appreciably less than girls. Wollner (1949), finding that among seventh, eighth and ninth grade children, the boys and girls alike borrowed an average of 16.6 books a year from the school library, agrees with the view put forward by Lehman and Witty that American boys tend to disclaim any great interest in reading because cultural influences dictate that reading be considered a feminine pursuit. This view is not unknown in Britain in certain classes of society, and it may go some way to explain the evidence adduced by every British investigator in this field, that girls more readily confess to enjoying reading, and in fact read more, than boys.

Of the 555 children who were members of Llanfair Public Library, 43 per cent were boys, 57 per cent were girls.[1] This agrees fairly closely with evidence found elsewhere, and notably in Glasgow, where of members of the Public Library, 64 per cent proved to be girls.[2] From Figure 3 it will be seen that only among the nine-year-olds does the percentage of boys joining the Library exceed that of the girls. This is the only time at which more than half the boys make use of the Library, whereas at least one half of all the girls are members after the age of six, and among the ten-year-olds the proportion rises to its peak of 89 per cent. This evidence supports the majority opinion that more girls than boys give their leisure-time to reading. There are

---

[1] The difference is highly significant ; Chi Square 33.6, P <.001.
[2] Dunlop, Doris C., 1949. Page 95.

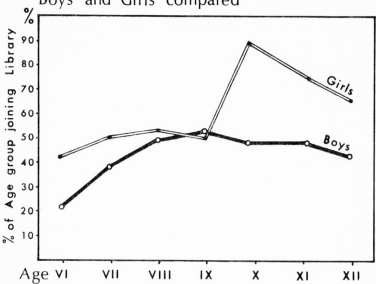

Figure 3

LIBRARY MEMBERSHIP AT EACH AGE

Boys and Girls compared

some discrepancies between this and the evidence of the Sheffield Public Libraries' Survey of 1938 that the number of readers rises (more slowly in the case of girls than boys) from the age of seven to ten, which is the peak for both sexes, with a preponderance of girls at all ages.[1] There is disagreement as to what happens between the ages of nine and ten, when from the present data it appears membership rises startlingly among the girls but begins to fall away among the boys. It may be that purely local factors are involved. It is possible, for instance, that the provision of books at Llanfair, excellently designed to meet the needs of boys and girls alike up to the age of nine, and of the girls beyond that age, is rather less successful in catering for the boys of ten. This can easily happen since, as will appear later, the tastes of boys and girls are very similar in early childhood, but the boys tend to develop specifically masculine interests at about the age of

[1]Quoted by Dunlop. P. 87.

nine, whereas essentially feminine tastes in books are not evinced by the girls until about the age of ten.

There are, of course, other possibilities. It would be surprising if, in the twenty years which separate the Sheffield enquiry and the present one, children's reading habits had not undergone some change. Dunlop, noting that among Glasgow children in 1947 membership of the Library was highest among the twelve- and thirteen-year-olds, speculates as to whether the war and the consequent decline in standards of reading achievement among children might account for the discrepancy between her findings and those of the Sheffield survey of 1938.[1] Standards of reading are now thought to have recovered from the set-back brought on by the war, and it may be because of this that the peak age observed in 1958 is closer to that found in 1938 than in 1947.

This explanation is based on the assumption, for which there is a good deal of evidence, that voluntary reading is related to reading achievement. There are grounds for believing that girls are generally superior to boys in reading ability, and it is reasonable to see a connection between this and the fact that more girls than boys adopt reading as a pastime. We have no means as yet of knowing whether, or to what extent, these differences are traceable to innate differences between the sexes ; it is certain, however, that cultural factors have some influence. It is the case, as has been mentioned, that reading tends to be regarded as an effeminate pursuit. More than that, the tradition still persists, though it may be on the wane, of permitting to boys more freedom than to girls to spend their leisure outside the home. Among Birmingham's adolescents, for example, it was found that the girls spent twice as many evenings at home as did the boys,[2] and that in consequence far more boys than girls, whether from lack of inclination or of time, gave no part of their spare time to reading books.

Obviously reading has to compete with other activities for a share of children's time, but such rival attractions are relatively few in early life. Indeed, while both boys and girls are confined, when not at school, almost entirely to the home, the latter may find it easier to spend their time in other ways than reading. It is much more natural for the girl than for the boy to share the mother's household tasks,

[1]Dunlop, p. 88.
[2]Westhill Training College : 1950. "80,000 Adolescents".

cleaning, mending, cooking, nursing. The boy has fewer opportunities of joining in his father's activities, and less incentive to remain indoors. Many, of course, while they are young are obliged by their parents to spend their evenings in the house, and for these reading may be the only attractive occupation available. This is probably why the boys who join the Library before the age of eight are on the whole more assiduous readers than the girls. It will be seen from Figure 4 that the average rate of borrowing by the boys who join the Library declines slightly between six and eight, then more perceptibly until the age of

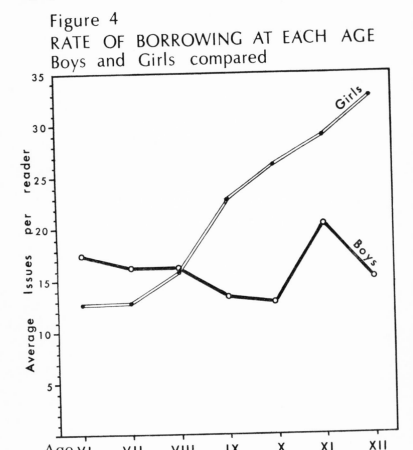

Figure 4
RATE OF BORROWING AT EACH AGE
Boys and Girls compared

ten.[1] Membership of the Library among the boys tends to increase until the age of nine, and it may be that the later recruits are on the whole less enthusiastic readers than the earlier ones, but it is significant that rising membership among the girls brings about no diminution in the rate of borrowing. The explanation seems to be that the boys as they grow older, and especially between eight and ten, are free to pursue out-door activities which are more attractive to them than reading, while the girls, still largely confined to the home but increasingly dissatisfied with the occupations in which they have hitherto engaged, turn more and more to reading. It is evident that the girls gain their freedom somewhat later than the boys, and it is not until after the age of ten that the numbers joining the Library decline, and even then the rate of borrowing on the part of those who remain continues to rise.

These fluctuations in membership and in rate of borrowing serve as forcible reminders that for children reading is at best a substitute for practical experience and personal involvement. Children therefore tend to read most in those periods in their lives when they find themselves shut off from fresh experiences. Emancipation from constant parental surveillance, coming earlier for the boys than for the girls, entry into secondary schools, and escape from childhood into adolescence, each of these brings with it a whole field of new activities and experiences, but in the period of mounting expectancy and frustration which precedes each one, it happens either that more children have recourse to reading or that those who already have the habit read more avidly.

[1]Confidence limits are given in Appendix, Table 2.

CHAPTER II

FICTION AND NON-FICTION

M ORE than eleven thousand books were issued from the Library in the course of the year to the children concerned in this enquiry, and in the overwhelming majority of cases the readers who had borrowed them claimed to have enjoyed them. Asked to express on a five-point scale approval or disapproval of each book they had taken out, they gave the highest rating, meaning that they had thoroughly enjoyed the book and would willingly read it again, to no less than 44 per cent of their selections ; of less than 7 per cent did they express positive dislike. The books they take home from the Library are obviously suited to their tastes, and it should therefore be possible, by examining the books issued, to gain some knowledge of what children are looking for in books, and of the way in which their interests alter as they grow. Such information is clearly relevant to the task of catering for children's needs and promoting healthy reading.

There have been many attempts to discover what children like to read. It is one thing, however, to amass an enormous amount of data about books which children have read or say they have enjoyed, but it is quite another matter to convey this information to others as meaningfully as possible. One method of ordering the evidence so that it reveals its significance is to ask the readers to rank the books or authors they have read in order of preference, and from the resulting votes to compile a list of those in the top ten or twelve places in the poll. Apart from the difficulty of deciding whether to give the same weight to the opinion of a child who has read only one book as to that of one who has read a hundred, there is the further drawback that the field is so large that even the most popular titles and authors attract only a very small proportion of the total votes cast. This also applies when the list is based, not on expressed preference, but on the number of people who can be taken to have read each book or author. Nearly two thousand different titles were issued by the Library at least once in the year ; since the total number of issues was a little over eleven thousand, each book was read on an average by fewer than six readers, and these not necessarily of the same age. Even those which were in very great demand were rarely borrowed more than twenty-five or thirty times, an inconsiderable proportion of the total number of issues, and it might be quite misleading to attach a great deal of significance to variations which must inevitably be extremely small. To know that books by Hans Andersen were borrowed on twenty-three and those of the Grimm brothers on twenty-two occasions, allows us neither to draw conclusions about the eleven thousand other books they borrowed, nor to say with any certainty that the former holds more appeal for children than the latter.

Jenkinson is among those who have adopted the procedure of compiling lists of popular books and authors based on children's declared preferences. One example may serve to illustrate some of the limitations of this method. Among the authors popular among twelve-year-old Senior school boys,[1] Dickens heads the list with 38 votes, while John Buchan comes seventh with five ; between them come R. L. Stevenson, Defoe, Thomas Hughes with *Tom Brown's Schooldays*, Kingsley, and Rider Haggard. Quite apart from the fact that Defoe, for instance, gains third place in the list with only twelve votes, teachers and librarians are struck by the apparent popularity of classic writers among relatively ungifted children. So totally at variance is this with their observations and experience that they may be forgiven for thinking that the children have set out deliberately to mislead. This may, of course, be true, but in any case the fact that a title or an author is well-known is itself sufficient to ensure that a relatively large number of children will have read his books, and if, as not infrequently it happens, a famous writer writes good books, many of those who read them will enjoy them, even though they habitually read much less exalted stuff. In other words, this list tells us more about the quality of Dickens as a writer than about children's tastes in books. Even so, it is as well that we should be reminded that writers such as Dickens have an immeasurably stronger appeal for their readers, few though they be, than the hundred run-of-the-mill writers who capture the great majority.

Other investigators have produced lists of the authors or books which have attracted the largest numbers of readers, and have used three main sources of information for this purpose. Carsley (1957) is one who employs the children's own records of the books they have read

---

[1]Jenkinson (1940), p. 71.

in the previous month ; the Child Readership Survey (1951) carried out by the British Research Bureau and Market Information Services is based on the sales of children's books ; Scanlan (1948) produces a list of the one hundred books most frequently taken from the shelves of the public libraries of St. Paul in the United States in the course of a year. These lists are alike—and in this they contrast sharply with that of Jenkinson—in that books of recent publication are predominant. The majority of those listed by Scanlan, for example, proved to have been published later than 1940, and are therefore unlikely to be familiar to adults, certainly outside the country of their origin. Apart from what can be gleaned from the titles, these lists provide very little insight into the kinds of books that children like to read, nor can there be any assurance that their authors will continue to be popular for more than a very short time. With the great increase since the second world war in the number of children's books being published, many new writers have enjoyed a brief period of popularity, while the accepted children's classics have fallen into neglect.

Though individual books and authors do not often remain long in vogue, the underlying tastes and interests of children, it may be supposed, are relatively constant.[1]   The majority of investigators have therefore attempted some system of classifying the books they find to be popular with children. The problem in devising such a system is to decide upon the criteria to be adopted in allocating books to different classes. Two books may be alike in one respect and dissimilar in another. From one standpoint, therefore, they may be regarded as belonging to the same class, but from another standpoint as belonging to different classes. This does not matter, as long as each book is judged from the same standpoint, or if the categories used are such that no book can belong to more than one. In practice, however, no-one, so far as we have been able to discover, has devised a completely consistent system of classifying children's books. Categories such as Fairy Stories, Historical Stories, School Stories, Adventure Stories, which have been adopted by nearly every investigator, are obviously extremely imprecise. To what category should be allocated, for example, a book which has a school setting, an historical background and an adventurous plot ? Very often, it is the best of children's

---

[1]Sward and Harris (1952), for example, find that the predominant themes in children's magazines changed very little between 1873 and 1933.

books which defy classification. All too many others are written to a
ready-made formula and are therefore easily allocated, but it is
difficult to find an objective criterion for dealing with such hybrids as
Fourth Form Detectives or *School in Space*.

While there is bound to be ambiguity in cases of this sort, it seemed
nevertheless worth trying to assign every book which had been
borrowed at least once to a class which underlined its salient features.
In any case, no other course seems practicable, since of the two thousand
or so books among which these children made their choices no more
than sixty[1] are likely to be well-known to adult readers, and these
accounted for less than two per cent of the total number of issues.
This makes it obvious, incidentally, that the children of today, at
least up to the age of twelve, are drawn far more to the works of
contemporary writers than to the classics.[2] The system of classification
adopted differs only in detail and not in principle from systems employed by others in this field. The books are divided into twelve main
groups, based for the most part on differences in plot. Thus a book
is deemed to be a School Story, not by virtue of its location, but
because it deals with characters involved in school relationships and
school activities. Were it to deal with the activities of characters
engaged in detecting crime, it would be classed as a Mystery story,
notwithstanding its setting. There are three exceptions to this:
Puppet stories, Fairy stories and Animal stories are distinguished not by
plot but by the kind of characters they deal with. From the standpoint
of plot, a story involving toys, fairies or animals might be regarded as a
Family Story, an Adventure Story, a School Story or any other kind
of story. In practice, however, because it is the nature of the characters
rather than of the plot which attracts the children who read these
kinds of book, it would be quite misleading to classify them otherwise.
In general, therefore, in assigning a book to a particular class, an
attempt is made to view it from the standpoint of the child trying to
decide whether it is the kind of book he likes to read, and to stress that
aspect to which the child considering that book is likely to pay most
attention.

---

[1] See Appendix, Table 4.
[2] A survey by Bethnal Green Public Library (1946) suggests that between
1939 and 1946 writers of light fiction such as Enid Blyton have gained ground
with children at the expense of authors such as Dickens, Lewis Carroll and
Mark Twain.

Figure 5 ANALYSIS OF ISSUES

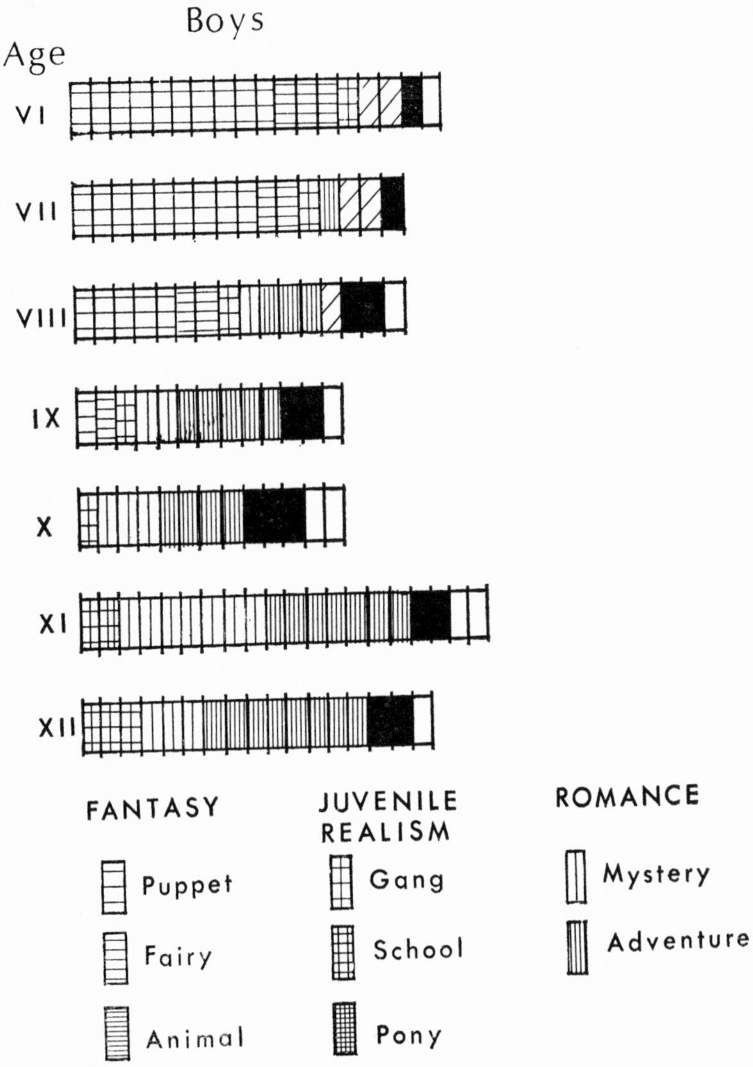

Boys

ACCORDING TO TYPES

Girls

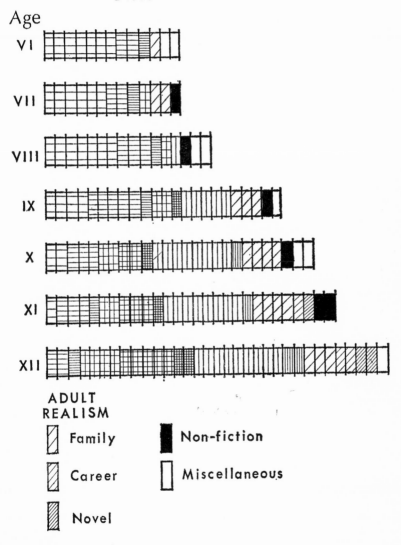

Age

VI

VII

VIII

IX

X

XI

XII

ADULT
REALISM

Family   Non-fiction

Career   Miscellaneous

Novel

Figure 5[1] illustrates the way in which the books selected by children at different ages are distributed among the various classes. To take as an illustration the girls' reading, it is clear that as the average number of books borrowed rises from 13 at the age of six to 33 at the age of twelve, so the variety of books selected enormously increases ; the average of 33 books issued to the twelve-year-olds is made up of 2 Fairy stories, 1 Animal, 4 Gang, 5 School, 2 Pony, 9 Mystery, 2 Adventure, 2 Careers stories and 2 Adolescent Novels, and another 1 which might belong to any of these classes.

Before going on to consider the extent to which each type of books appeals to boys and girls at different ages, it might be as well to look for a moment at the overall pattern of development that is revealed. It seems, for instance, that sex differences in reading interests are very small before the age of eight. It is true that the taste for Adventure stories, which may be regarded as essentially masculine, emerges very early, but otherwise the books taken out by the boys of six and seven are very much the same as those borrowed by the girls. By the age of nine, the differences are quite considerable. The Adventure Stories so attractive to the boys are utterly neglected by the girls, while the Puppet and Fairy stories, which still form a considerable proportion of those read by the girls, have almost entirely fallen out of favour with the boys. By the age of ten, the main interest which the boys share with the girls is in the Mystery story, though in catering for the tastes of a mixed class of children of this age, it might be possible to find Gang stories, Adventure stories, and works of non-fiction which appeal to both sexes.

What is perhaps most striking is the lack of variety in the reading of the boys compared with that of the girls. One has the strong impression that, other than in the fields of the Adventure story and the Mystery, there is a serious shortage of books suitable for boys, and that this accounts in part for the comparative lack of interest in reading on the part of the boys beyond the age of nine. Whether it is that the girls are more fortunate in this respect, or that they make better use of the books available to them, it is quite evident that the boys' reading is much more limited in its range. It would seem that when they are not reading for information, they read almost exclusively for what might be termed escapist reasons, and leave wide reaches of experience

---

[1]See also Appendix, Tables 3a and 3b.

unexplored, at least in books. Reading that has so little bearing on the lives they live cannot but seem ultimately profitless even to themselves, and it is small wonder that they are so much less interested in books than are the girls. It must be apparent that if boys are to develop an enduring interest in books and a true appreciation of their worth, they need to be aware, from an early age, that books can enormously extend their own experience and illuminate every aspect of their lives. And this means that above all their reading should be varied.

Puppet Stories

At first sight there seems to be little variety in the reading of the average child of six. Apart from a small minority, the books issued to boys and girls of this age are either Puppet or Fairy stories. In fact, however, books belonging to these two classes are alike only in that they are peopled by humanised animals and toys—dolls, bunnies, engines, in the one case, or gnomes, elves and fairies in the other. In their themes, however, they can be as varied as life itself; these puppet figures are shown meeting the vicissitudes of school life, family life, love, marriage, parenthood, danger, even war, and through them children can enjoy a range of vicarious experience almost as wide as that offered by adult literature. The essential difference between this and adult literature is that the characters, while possessing human attributes, wear some obviously fictitious guise, as if to reassure their readers of their unreality.

Stories in which animals play human roles are at least as old as Aesop's Fables, popular in this country since Caxton's edition of 1484, and still among the Toy stories borrowed by these children from the library. More light-hearted fables ot this kind, written specially for children, were first produced in the eighteenth century by L'Estrange, Croxall and Dodsley, but it is the illustrated tales of Beatrix Potter, first published in the last century, which are today the best-known examples of this genre.[1] Still highly popular, as is shown by the fact that they were issued more than fifty times, they have attracted a number of modern imitators, of whom Noel Barr, Jane Pilgrim, and

---

[1]Darton (1932) gives an absorbing account of the history of children's books in England. On this, on Meigs (1956), Smith, L. H. (1953) and Eyre (1952), I have relied heavily for the historical details presented in this chapter.

A. J. MacGregor in collaboration with W. Perring, are the most prolific.

In the Picture Book form associated with the name of Beatrix Potter, these tales are chiefly read by children up to the age of seven, but in the more demanding form popularised in 1880 by Joel Chandler Harris, American author of the Uncle Remus tales, Aesopian fables are still among the books borrowed by the boys at nine, and by the girls at eleven years of age. Harris himself claims five readers only, Kenneth Grahame four, but their more modern successors, Alison Uttley, author of the stories of Sam Pig, and Rodney Bennett, creator of the mouse heroine, Little Miss Pink, have a considerable following.

The origin of story-books in which the leading roles are borne by toys is not easy to trace, but it is certainly no later than the appearance in this country, in Mary Howitt's translation of 1846, of Hans Andersen's *Wonderful Stories for Children*, which included the tale of the Little Tin Soldier. The golliwog first appeared in print in 1895, in a story by Florence and Bertha Upton, and is still familiar to these children as a minor character in Enid Blyton's Noddy books, while Teddy Bear, who made his debut shortly after, is chiefly known through the stories of Mrs. H. C. Cradock. A. A. Milne is perhaps the most distinguished writer of this kind of book, but Winnie the Pooh has yielded in the esteem of these children to Muffin the Mule in the stories of Ann Hogarth and Annette Mills, and to Muriel Levy's Wonk.

In children's books of recent times human attributes have been extended to cars, lorries, tractors, trains, ships, helicopters, steam-shovels and sky-scrapers. They are commonly produced as picture books in which print has only a minor part, and in this form they are widely read up to the age of seven, but more difficult books such as those of Elizabeth Chapman about Marmaduke the Lorry are read by boys up to the age of nine and by girls even later. Not unnaturally, perhaps, the boys tend to prefer stories about mechanical toys of this kind to the dolls and toy animals favoured by the girls, but Puppet stories of one sort or another form more than a half of the books borrowed at the age of six by boys and girls alike, declining by the age of nine to 6 per cent among the boys, 17 per cent among the girls.[1]

---

[1] The difference is highly significant. Chi Square 42.4 ; $P < .001$.

Fairy Stories

Already, at the age of six, there are signs of a growing interest in characters more recognisably human than those of Puppet stories. Nursery rhymes make their first appearance among books borrowed at this age. Some at least of the jingles and catches still popular in this form are thought originally to have lampooned real political figures and events. The earliest collection known, *Tom Thumb's Pretty Song Book*, edited by N. Lovechild and published by M. Cooper, appeared in 1774, while another, *Mother Goose's Melody*, is believed to have been compiled by Goldsmith for John Newbery, the first publisher of children's books. The same rhymes, in modern coloured editions, still attract a number of these children, but it is the Fairy story that stands next to the Puppet story in popularity at this age. This, too, has a long history. Perrault's *Histoires ou Contes du temps passé, avec des Moralitez*, published in 1698, refurbished for French courtly taste the stories told by peasants to their children. *Sleeping Beauty, Little Red Riding Hood, Puss in Boots* and *Cinderella* were speedily translated into English, but at this stage they were not mainly intended for children. The *Kindermarchen* of the brothers Grimm appeared in German between 1812 and 1824, and were introduced to England shortly after by Ruskin as *Household Tales*, translated by Edgar Taylor and illustrated by Cruikshank, while Andersen's *Wonderful Stories for Children* appeared in 1846.

All these stories, in modern versions closely following the originals, are still widely read, as are the *Fairy Books* compiled by Andrew Lang in the last century, and also appear, very much simplified, in picture-book editions intended for the very young. Even so, tales of this kind, with their origins in folk-lore, form only a part of the Fairy stories read by children. Many others trace their lineage through Kipling's *Rewards and Fairies* (1926) and *Puck of Pook's Hill* (1906), Lewis Carroll's *Alice's Adventure in Wonderland* (1865), Kingsley's *Water Babies* (1863) back to William Roscoe's *The Butterfly's Ball* (1807). These are works of original invention, though the gnomes, elves and fairies with which they are peopled form part of a native tradition obscurely linked with the Arthurian legend. It was known to Chaucer's Wife of Bath, Shakespeare drew upon it for his *Midsummer Night's Dream*, and vestiges of it still remain in local legends, both in England and in Wales. The modern elf and gnome, as they appear, for example, in Enid Blyton's stories, though they belong to the same twilit, magical world, have nothing of the elemental quality of Puck, Oberon and Titania ; instead, they are shy, fragile and laughter-loving, idealised children possessing magical power.   There is a world of difference, too, between these and the supernatural beings who people the stories of C. S. Lewis and of J. R. R. Tolkien, and between these and Mary Norton's Borrowers or Barbara Euphan Todd's Worzel Gummidge.   Almost the only thing they have in common is the element of magic, of the supernatural, and this is the sole criterion distinguishing books which have been classed as Fairy Stories.   These range, therefore, from simple picture-books to the very difficult, and include works as widely different as those of Perrault, Enid Blyton and Tolkien.

Roughly one-sixth of all the books borrowed by the boys of six belong to this class, but they decline very rapidly in popularity until they are virtually ignored by boys aged ten.   In contrast, the girls' interest in stories of this kind is at its peak among the nine-year-olds and remains quite strong even among those of twelve.   It must be remembered, of course, that the picture-book versions chosen by the six-year-olds gradually give way to more demanding books, and at the same time the innocuous fairy story of the kind written by Enid Blyton tends to be pushed out of favour among the older children by more sophisticated stories such as those of Perrault and Andrew Lang, and stories of magical events in a contemporary setting by authors such as Barbara Euphan Todd and P. L. Travers.

Animal Stories

In the Puppet story and the Fairy story, the characters, however disguised, bear some obvious sign of their essential humanity ; by their physical appearance, their dress, their habits or their speech, they invite their readers to regard them as human beings.   In the Animal story, on the other hand, the characters around whom the action revolves wear no disguise ; they are animals—horses, dolphins, otters, salmon, birds—appearing as themselves, and claiming no special affinity with human beings.   In some cases, they are imagined as being capable of speech, and their authors do not always avoid, or even try to avoid, endowing them with human thoughts and feelings ; but externally their appearance, their activities and their way of life are those of animals.   Although their authors do not insist on any resemblances between these animals and human beings, children reading, let us say, the story of a pony stolen from its owner and ill-treated by strangers before finally being restored, cannot but draw parallels from what they know of human life, or from their own experience. While in one sense the Animal story is more realistic than the Puppet or the Fairy story, in another sense it is, like them, an allegory in which human beings appear in disguise. The difference is, of course, that in the Animal story it is the reader, not the author, who humanises the characters.

Essentially an Animal story is the fictional biography, or sometimes the autobiography, of an animal, and is distinguishable from other kinds of books in which animals appear in that the animal itself is at the centre of the plot, rather than any human beings with whom it may be related. In some stories, the fictional element is exiguous, while in others fantasy is given full rein. At the one extreme Gladys Taylor's *The Swallows and Selina* is virtually a book of nature study, while at the other there is little to distinguish the animals in Dodie Smith's *The Hundred and One Dalmations* from those of Beatrix Potter. The typical Animal story avoids both extremes, and is more akin to Anna Sewell's *Black Beauty*, Jack London's *Call of the Wild*, or Kipling's *Thy Servant, a Dog*. All these were occasionally borrowed, but modern stories such as Thomas C. Hinkle's *Tan* and D. Broome's *Circus Pony*, were more popular.

The girls begin to borrow books of this kind at the age of six, and continue to read an average of one a year throughout this period except at the age of ten. Oddly enough, the boys very rarely borrow stories of this sort[1] ; the older ones show some interest in stories such as J. O'Brien's *Silver Chief*, an adventurous tale not unlike *The Call of the Wild*, but few of them are greatly attracted to the more sentimental Animal stories, similar to *Black Beauty*, which interest the girls. This neatly illustrates the major difference between the boys and girls as readers : the former are attracted mainly by stories of sensational events, the latter by accounts of personal relationships.

Gang Stories

The three types of story hitherto considered, the Puppet, the Fairy and, to a lesser degree, the Animal story, belong essentially to the Infant school period or to early childhood. They continue to be read,

---

[1]This difference is significant. Chi Square 6.28 ; P<.02.

particularly by the girls, up to the age of twelve, but in decreasing numbers. They are gradually ousted by other kinds of books which are more closely concerned with the interests and activities of children in the pre-pubertal stage. The first of these kinds to make its appearance is the Gang story, which enjoys a modest popularity among the six-year-old boys and which thereafter is borrowed in ever increasing numbers by both boys and girls at least until the age of twelve. Almost alone among all the kinds of books which children read, it attracts boys and girls alike at every age, and for that reason deserves close attention. It is important for another reason also : an awakening interest in stories of this kind marks the beginning of a new and more realistic phase in the development of the child as a reader.

An atmosphere of reality is perhaps the most distinctive feature of stories belonging to this class. The *milieu* is the world of the peer group, in which adults, when not excluded entirely, occupy only very minor roles, and the values, rules and sanctions that prevail derive, not from the adult world, but from the gang. To that extent, these stories give fanciful expression to the growing child's rebellion against adult domination, but within the limits of the juvenile world which they describe, the characters are not unlifelike, nor are their activities far-fetched. Many are tales of youthful mischief, of which those of Richmal Crompton are still perhaps the best known and most popular, but in others the children are animated not so much by rebelliousness, as by the need for independence and responsibility. In Kathleen Fidler's *St. Jonathan's in the Country*, for example, a number of children exert themselves on behalf of a hospital for orphans established in the Lancashire countryside, while in Monica Edwards' *Storm Ahead*, when floods overtake a small fishing village nearby, the boys and girls take part beside their elders in the work of rescue and relief. In nearly all these stories there is an element of adventure, though not such as to strain belief, but the emphasis is less upon the physical exploits than on personal and social relationships within the group, or between the group and the community. Also belonging to this class are the works of Arthur Ransome and his many successors. Ransome himself began to write in 1930, and his tales of the exploits of groups of children calling themselves the Swallows and the Amazons set a fashion in children's books which has endured to this day. Though the popularity of Ransome's stories is perhaps now on the wane, other writers, George E. Haley and Gilbert Hackforth-Jones notable among them, have employed his device of setting his characters afloat on rivers, lakes and coastal waters to enjoy completely credible and legitimate adventures.

School Stories

Akin to the Gang story is the School story. Like the former, it is concerned with activities, relationships and values which belong essentially to a world of children, and this world it portrays in reasonably life-like and credible terms. Children's mischief is the theme of many of the School stories popular today, but the earliest of the species, *Tom Brown's Schooldays* by Thomas Hughes (1856) and Frederic W. Farrar's *Eric, or Little by Little ; a Tale of Roslyn School* (1858) were written in a different, more moralising vein. Nearer in spirit to the school-boys of modern fiction are the characters of the stories written for *The Boys' Own Paper* by Talbot Baines Reed between 1879 and 1893, or of Kipling's *Stalky and Co.*, published in 1899. The Jennings books of Anthony Buckeridge belong to this tradition, but in these the main characters are rather younger than was usual in earlier School stories, and they seem to be designed to appeal to rather younger readers.

School stories, in any case, have so far fallen out of favour among the boys as to represent little more than one per cent of all their borrowings. Among the girls, however, they are held in high esteem. The taste for stories of this kind appears rather suddenly towards the end of primary school life, and grows rapidly in the next few years. Even so, the School story for girls appears to be evolving in directions parallel to those followed earlier by School books for boys. The works of Angela Brazil, Margaret Biggs and Nancy Breary, which broadly speaking are counter-parts of those of Talbot Baines Reed, Kipling and Frank Richards, seem to be yielding to those of Enid Blyton, which, like those of Anthony Buckeridge, are concerned with younger characters and are designed for younger readers than was formerly the case. Other writers make no pretence of giving a credible account of school life ; the schools themselves are often situated in Switzerland or Skye, or other even more romantic places, their regime is often unorthodox in the extreme, and their pupils include a surprising number of heiresses, princesses and film-stars in disguise. Many stories of this sort, though they have a school background, are not essentially concerned with school activities or with the responses children make to the school situation, and are therefore more fitly classified as Mystery or Adventure stories. The hall-mark of the School story, as of the Gang story, is its concern with fairly life-like children in fairly credible situations.

Pony Stories

The Gang Story and the School Story portray children engaged in activities proper to children and involved in relationships with others of their kind. The Pony Story is like both in these respects. The most popular among the stories of this type, those of Christine, Diana and Josephine Pullein-Thompson, describe the pleasures and excitement of the hunt and the gymkhana, but implicit in them is the suggestion that the ownership of a pony and the ability to ride are keys to friendship with other children. The standard of horsemanship is the criterion by which these children judge and are judged, and in striving to be more proficient, they make themselves acceptable to their fellows. Even in these stories, however, the horse is usually more than a mere symbol of status in the peer group ; a strong sense of intimacy is sometimes shown to exist between animal and owner, and the child is depicted as finding in its relations with an animal the love and affection which it has not found in its relationships with human beings. Pet animals appear, of course, in children's stories of all kinds, but in Pony stories, and in others similar to them in spirit but involving dogs or other animals, the relationship between the animal and the child forms the central theme. In some cases, the child and the animal are beset by similar problems and find their way together to similar solutions. Both pony and child may have become suspicious and unfriendly as a result of the ill-treatment they have suffered ; the trust that grows up between them enables them to win success at the horse-show, thus ensuring for the animal a good home, and for the child the affection of parents and friends.

In many of these Pony stories, therefore, an emotional or psychological theme underlies, and runs parallel to, the superficial account of horses and horsemanship. Not surprisingly, then, the boys show little interest in these stories, but the girls are attracted to them from about the age of nine. Certain of these stories appeal particularly to the twelve-year-olds, because the psychological sub-plot concerns the emotional development of an adolescent girl. In D. V. S. Jackson's *Bluebird*, for example, the heroine overcomes her fears of the horse, and learns to accept risk and danger as the price to be paid for the happiness that horsemanship can bring. At the same time this experience makes her prepared to give up the security of childhood and to conquer her fear of the young man who offers her his love. In *The Silver Quest* by Elizabeth Bleecker Meigs, the horse is again given a symbolic value. Chela, approaching adolescence on her grand-father's Mexican ranch, befriends a wild silver stallion, last of a breed introduced by a national hero as a symbol of the freedom for which he had fought in vain. She mends the horse's broken leg, and, resisting the temptation to make the horse her faithful slave, sets it at liberty. In recognition of her unpossessive love, the horse returns to her once before escaping to the wilds, and the girl is made aware of love as the means of freedom and fulfilment.

Mystery Stories

Only in the superficial appurtenances of the plot do these stories of Meigs or Jackson resemble the Pony stories of the Pullein-Thompsons, and an even wider gulf separates them from the School stories of Enid Blyton and the Gang stories of Arthur Ransome. Despite these differences and the inherent weakness they reveal in this and any other system of classifying books, School, Gang and Pony stories are alike in that they deal with the activities and preoccupations of young-sters not vastly different from their readers. In this they are distinguish-able from books which have been classed as Mystery stories. These appeal to their readers, not because the characters they portray are subject to the same difficulties and limitations as themselves, but because the characters, though children, enjoy experiences considerably more eventful and exciting than are conceivable in real life.

Catherine Sinclair's *Holiday House*, which in 1863 recounted the exploits of a group of children left free to pursue their own devices, is in some respects the fore-runner of stories of this kind. It is notable for introducing into children's books the first of the tolerant grand-parents and jolly uncles who almost unfailingly appear in the Mystery stories of today. The essential ingredient in these stories, the invest-igating by children of suspicious adult behaviour, appears, probably for the first time in children's books, in Mark Twain's *Tom Sawyer* (1876), though the smugglers, spies and gipsies who are the villains of more recent books are usually less murderous than Injun Joe, and the children much more masters of the situation than are Tom Sawyer and Huckleberry Finn. It is characteristic of these stories that, in spite of the dangers and difficulties which the children incur, the atmosphere is one of gaiety and enjoyment rather than of fear and anxiety. This emphasises the element of wish-fulfilment, of escapism, in stories of this type, an element which is especially noticeable in the *Famous Five* and *Secret Seven* stories of Enid Blyton, which are certainly the most widely read of all.

The enormous popularity enjoyed by these and other stories like them calls for explanation. Mystery stories make their first appearance in appreciable numbers among the borrowings of the eight-year-olds, and thereafter are read in increasing numbers until the age of eleven, when their appeal for the boys, though not for the girls, begins to wane. At the peak of their popularity, they form roughly a third of all the books issued to the boys and girls alike. It is obvious therefore that these stories respond to needs which are extremely widespread among children of this age, and that an examination of these stories may yield clues as to what these needs may be. The most important perhaps is the need felt by the child to be accepted by his fellows. Recognising the importance of this as a motive for reading, Enid Blyton invites her readers to apply for membership of the "Secret Seven Society". Even without this invitation children certainly identify themselves with members of the gang, and Enid Blyton has made this easier by including in her gangs children of different ages and of either sex. These stories cater too for the child's need to be freed occasionally from parental supervision, and to assert his independence and self-reliance. It is obvious also that this concern with mysteries reflects the child's awareness that in real life there are mysteries from which he is excluded, as it seems to him, by a conspiracy of silence on the part of adults. And finally, the child approaching adolescence asserts his claim to be considered on terms of equality with adults, a claim seldom upheld in real life, but in these books, where the children invariably get the better of the adults, acknowledged in full.

Adventure Stories

The Adventure story meets many of the same psychological needs, but the books in this class differ from those of the Mystery in that the *milieu* is more adult, the incidents more violent, and the atmosphere more tense. The distinctions between the two are often small, but the holiday atmosphere which almost invariably prevails in the Mystery story is quite different from the air of anxiety and tension which pervades the Adventure story. It is partly for this reason, no doubt, that they appeal more strongly to the boys than to the girls, and to older rather than to younger children, but it is also the case that they are almost all intended for the older boys, since girls seldom appear in these stories, and the central characters are nearly always youths or young men. Even so, from about the age of ten, the girls themselves borrow books belonging to this category, though only at the age of twelve does the average reach two books a year. In contrast, they form a substantial proportion of the books borrowed by the boys from the age of seven, while at the age of nine and upwards they are more widely read than any other kind of book.

Tales of heroism existed long before any written language was invented. In Europe, the *chansons de geste* popular throughout the Middle Ages had their origin in the much older oral traditions that arose from historical events, and stories similar in origin, *Guy of Warwick, Bevis of Hampton, Havelock the Dane, Robin Hood* and *King Arthur*, were among the first to come from Caxton's press after 1484. Of these, the tales of Robin Hood and King Arthur still claim a number of readers, and to these have been added many other stories by historical novelists from Sir Walter Scott to Henry Treece.

While these authors have looked to the past for the source of their material, others have given their stories a contemporary setting, or, following the example of Jules Verne and H. G. Wells, have looked into the future for subjects for Adventure stories. The basic theme remains the same, however : the ultimate triumph, through physical force, of the good over the bad. At first sight, there are only superficial differences between R. L. Stevenson's *Treasure Island* and Percy F. Westerman's *The Lure of the Lagoon*, or between Buchan's *Prester John* and W. E. John's *Biggles and the Black Raider* ; almost the only innovation is in the introduction of modern settings and inventions. Naturally enough, children like their stories to appear up-to-date, but it is among readers of Adventure stories that the demand for novelty is most vociferous. As a result, writers of Adventure stories appear to be engaged in an unending struggle to keep abreast of the times. Eric Leyland, one of the most prolific authors of Adventure books for boys, has written of pirates and of Cowboys and Indians, but by far the most popular of his books are those dealing with a group of young men in modern times, equipped with automatics, fast cars and aeroplanes, and dedicated to the task of hunting to destruction criminals and saboteurs in all corners of the earth. W. E. Johns, whose stories of adventure in the air have been enormously popular since World War II, has in recent years launched his heroes into outer space.

While at first sight these changes appear purely external and superficial, in fact the Adventure story of today is profoundly different in atmosphere and tone from the more reputable of its forerunners. A comparison between *Treasure Island*, for example, and almost any modern story of Space adventure, illustrates the point. The modern story, despite its bizarre and often horrific contents, rarely has on its readers the emotional impact of *Treasure Island*. It is sensational without being truly moving ; it may stretch the nerves, but does not stir the feelings. The reader of *Treasure Island* has no difficulty in recognising Jim Hawkins as a boy not unlike himself, and in seeing all the other characters, good and bad, as human beings of the kind he meets in daily life. The reactions of these characters to one another and to the situations in which they are involved are much the same as those which the reader has already observed in himself and in other people in parallel circumstances in real life. Because the fictitious characters and situations wear this air of familiarity, the reader responds to them *in propria persona*, so to speak. His feelings about them are his normal feelings, clarified, intensified, made more perceptive and articulate perhaps, but nevertheless compatible with his ordinary personal experience. Unlike Stevenson, the modern writer of Adventure stories tends in the search for constant novelty to stress the unfamiliar and outlandish ; settings tend to become more and more fantastic, incidents more and more sensational, characters less and less human. The reader's personal experience therefore gives no clue to the kind of emotional response that is appropriate to the fictitious situation. Reading of Long John Silver's downfall, for example, he responds with feelings of the same order as those he experienced, let us say, on hearing that the headmaster he disliked has had a serious accident, and he is confirmed in his reactions by the fact that he shares them with the hero, Jim Hawkins. His personal, human reactions are made to appear wildly inappropriate, however, in the face, let us say, of the destruction by lethal rays of a distant planet and all its monstrous inhabitants.

Many people have misgivings about the effects upon children of violence in comics, books, films and television programmes. Whether these fears are justified or not still remains uncertain, but in any case a clear distinction can be drawn between violence to which the reader is invited to respond in a fully human fashion—not only with excitement but with fear, not only with triumph but with pity—and that violence which is exploited solely for sensation, and which is intended to evoke a purely nervous, reflex reaction. The growing addiction of these boys to stories of Adventure is itself evidence of the fact that an appetite for thrills grows with what it feeds upon. Whether this is positively harmful in a moral sense may be open to doubt, but there can be little denying that the taste for Adventure stories tends to oust all interest in books better qualified to do what literature can supremely do : refine the sensibilities, educate the emotions, teach us to feel what it is like to be a human being.

Family Stories

Teachers in secondary schools generally agree that girls come to appreciate adult literature at an earlier age than do boys. Part of the explanation for this lies in the fact that, whereas boys are largely addicted to Mystery and Adventure stories in their voluntary reading, girls are accustomed to read from early childhood stories which have an affinity with adult novels in that they are concerned with personal relationships and emotional problems, and that their treatment of these themes is designed to convey an impression of realism and authenticity. These are the characteristics of the Family stories, which are rarely read by the boys above the age of eight, but remain in favour with the girls at least until the age of twelve. These stories deal with the activities of individuals in the home, and their relationships with other members of the family. They range from Picture books telling of the children's party in the nursery, to long and moving accounts of loneliness and deprivation such as *Oliver Twist* and *Uncle Tom's Cabin*. Although modern stories are rarely as harrowing as these, those which appeal to older children often have a vein of pathos. Joanna Spyri's *Heidi*, telling of an orphan's efforts to melt the heart of her obdurate grand-father, is extremely popular, as is Ian Serrailler's *The Silver Sword*, which tells of a family of children who make their way from war-time Poland to find their father and mother in Switzerland. Others, such as Enid Blyton's *The Queen Elizabeth Family* and

Grace James's *John and Mary* stories, are much more light-hearted and appeal mainly to the younger girls.

Among the Family stories are a number of day-to-day accounts of children's lives in which the story element is reduced to a minimum. Mrs. Molesworth's *Carrots : just a little boy*, published in 1876, is of this kind, but more popular today are fictional accounts of children living in foreign countries : Lois Lenski describes in *Judy's Journey* the life of the family of a migrant farm labourer in the United States ; *Oolak's Brother* by Bud Helmericks deals with an Eskimo family, while Andree Clair's *Moudaina* is the story of a negro boy in the Chad ; most popular of all among these children is Laura Ingalls Wilder's semi-autobiographical account of life in a log cabin in Wisconsin entitled *Little House in Big Woods*. In these, and to some degree in all Family stories, an attempt is made to present ordinary human beings, children especially, in domestic situations which, though sometimes unusual, are always natural and credible. Their main value for their readers lies in the fact that they portray people adapting themselves to circumstances and situations not totally unlike those with which they themselves are faced in daily life ; they present patterns of behaviour which the readers themselves might fittingly adopt. In short, these stories manifestly set out to show their readers how human life is or can be lived, and this is clearly what their readers desire to learn.

Careers Stories

The home obviously plays a more important part in the lives of girls than of boys, especially in the middle years of childhood, and this explains to some extent the lack of interest in Family stories among the boys. As children approach adolescence, however, they become increasingly preoccupied with the need to equip themselves to meet the demands of adult social life, to become independent of their parents and to associate on equal terms with adults in the world outside.

The Careers story, which caters quite specifically for young people at this stage in their development, is of very recent origin. Among the very first of its kind was Helen Dore Boylston's *Sue Barton, Student Nurse*, which remains extremely popular and has the characteristics peculiar to all stories belonging to this class. It conveys, within a fictional framework, a certain amount of useful guidance to readers contemplating a particular career. Far more important, however, than the factual information it provides is the account it gives of the central character's emotional problems and personal relations. The adolescent is shown making difficult choices, facing disappointment and failure, enduring rivalry and deceit, and often finding love and marriage. In stories, at least, nursing is easily the most popular career, but teaching, librarianship, secretarial work, and countless others have been treated in stories of this kind. It is evident, however, that the chief interest of their readers is not in the careers themselves, or in the factual details, but in the personal and psychological elements in the story. As evidence of this it may be said that children who read stories of this kind rarely restrict their choices to those dealing with one or two careers, but read Careers stories of every sort.

Books of this kind have been written for boys, but even these attract at least as many readers among the girls as among the boys. The great majority are designed for girls, and within the age-range considered here it is the girls alone who read them in any quantity. They are first attracted to them at about the age of eleven, and their interest grows stronger in the following year and probably persists for some years beyond. This growth of interest in Careers stories provides a very clear example of the way in which children's reading tastes reflect their emotional and psychological development, and illustrates how their reading sometimes prepares children to meet their own problems of adjustment. The Careers story is especially well adapted to serve this purpose because it deals in every-day language with quite undistinguished characters in contemporary situations. Its treatment even of love and courtship is deliberately prosaic and matter-of-fact, and this is the secret of its appeal to readers approaching adolescence, for whom these themes already have in any case strong emotional implications. This common-sense approach, though it inevitably deprives the Careers story of any distinction as literature, is reassuring to the reader since it implies that the anxieties and difficulties he or she experiences are normal to adolescents, and in any case surmountable.

Adolescent Novels

The matter-of-fact tone of the Careers story distinguishes it from what may be called the Adolescent Novel, of which Louisa M. Alcott's *Little Women* (1868) is an early and still popular example. Whereas the Careers story underlines the typicality of its characters and their situation, the Adolescent Novel lays more stress upon their singularity. The underlying theme in both is that of the adolescent's attempt to meet the demands of adult life, but the Adolescent Novel is less concerned with the practical than with the emotional, moral, or spiritual trials the individual undergoes. *Heidi grows up* and *Heidi's Children*, written by Charles Tritten as sequels to Joanna Spyri's *Heidi*, were often borrowed, as were L. M. Montgomery's *Chronicles of Avonlea, Anne of Green Gables, Anne of Avonlea* and others, but the most popular of all were those of Mabel Esther Allan, in which tone and atmosphere are appreciably more modern. Apart from the relative youth of the central characters, there is no great difference between these and adult novels of sentiment or of manners, and in practice it was found convenient to consider some of the few adult novels which these children read, notably Jane Austen's *Pride and Prejudice* and Thackeray's *Vanity Fair*, as belonging to this class.

Like the Careers story, the Adolescent Novel was borrowed almost exclusively by girls, rarely before the age of eleven but in increasing numbers at the age of twelve. Very few books of this kind appear to have been written with boys in view. The fact that in the majority the principal character is a female is itself enough to ensure that they will be read by very few boys, but even if this were not the case it is doubtful whether they would appeal strongly to them. It is sometimes said that girls achieve emotional maturity earlier than do boys. If such differences do in fact exist, they need not be attributed to biological factors. Generally, in our society, the role played by the daughter during childhood bears a closer correspondence to the role played by the mother than does the role of the son to that of the father. The girl commonly has her mother's company and shares her duties inside the home and out, and thereby serves a long and slow apprenticeship for adulthood and for her future responsibilities as wife and mother. Rarely, except perhaps in the case of the eldest son of a widowed mother, do the duties placed upon a boy fore-shadow the responsibilities he will meet, either in the home as a husband and a father, or outside as a worker, a neighbour and a citizen. For boys, the transition to adulthood is more abrupt, and they have little warning during childhood of the changes it entails. The Family story, the Careers story and the Adolescent Novel all deal with the individual as a social being, dependent upon, and responsible for, certain other human beings in the family or the world at large. For the girls, such themes are relevant, both to their immediate lives and to the lives they look forward to as adults ; the boys find little in them that applies to their present lives, nor as yet have they much reason to suppose that as adults they will be more concerned with questions of the sort. By convention and by training, the boy's affiliations and obligations are mainly to his peers, those of the girl to the family and community. Their reading both reflects and consolidates the difference.

Non-fiction

This contrast of outlook between the boys and girls is again apparent in their attitudes towards books other than of fiction. It is fairly well established that, both in childhood and in adolescence, boys read more non-fiction than do girls, but that for neither sex does non-fiction form more than a fairly small proportion of their total reading. Books of this kind account for roughly 12 per cent of the total number issued to the boys, for 5 per cent of those issued to the girls.[1] For the most part they deal with factual information, practical subjects, or general ideas, and as such hold little appeal for the girls, whose interest is mainly in the personal and human aspects of experience.

Non-fiction in the Junior Library is classified according to the Dewey Decimal system commonly in use in the public libraries of this country. The books most often borrowed, both by boys and girls, are those concerned with leisure pursuits (Dewey classification, 700—799), which make up roughly one-fifth of all the non-fiction borrowed.[2] Books on football, cricket, boxing, swimming, and camping attract the boys of eight and over, while those on horsemanship and tennis appeal chiefly to the girls. Books on indoor activities, drawing, acting, dancing, and, of course, knitting and embroidery, are borrowed for the most part by the girls, though the boys occasionally take out books dealing with woodwork and similar crafts. Children show little awareness at this stage of purely aesthetic considerations ; they are quite indifferent to books on the appreciation of art, music, sculpture and the like, but are attracted by books which offer possible outlets for activity.

Books on scientific topics (Dewey classification, 500—599) come next in order of popularity among both boys and girls. The great majority of the books they borrow deal with the natural sciences, with nature study and, especially, with animal life. Accounts of

---

[1]Highly significant. $P < .001$
[2]See Appendix, Table 5.

animals in the zoo attract children from the age of six, and their interest extends later to books on wild life, on animals and birds, and to a lesser extent fish and insects, of the countryside. Among the most popular of these are the books of G. Bramwell Evens, in which the naturalist, Romany, records his observations of wild life in the company of a young boy, Tim. Books on the mathematical and physical sciences, astronomy, chemistry and physics, are occasionally borrowed by the boys, but very rarely by the girls.

Books on the useful arts (Dewey classification, 600—699) are issued mainly to the boys, since the majority deal with technical and mechanical topics. The construction of ships, cars, locomotives and aeroplanes has great fascination for the boys, but among the books belonging to this category, only those which deal with the care of animals and other pets are borrowed in appreciable numbers by the girls. Books on the various public services, the army, navy, transport, the post-office and police (Dewey classification, 300—399) are again much more popular with the boys than with the girls. It is interesting to see, on the other hand, that books connected with religion (Dewey classification, 200—299) literary works (Dewey classification 800—899) and biographies all rank higher with the girls than with the boys. In their choice of books, whether fiction or non-fiction, the girls reveal their constant concern with personal relationships and inner experience, the boys their interest in the external world and in physical activity. It needs to be said again, perhaps, that this contrast is not necessarily associated with innate differences between the sexes. In recent times, anthropologists have shown that in one society the males may exhibit attitudes and modes of behaviour which in another society are characteristic of the females. There is a good deal of pressure, direct and indirect, upon the individual to conform to the pattern which the culture to which he or she belongs prescribes for each of the sexes. The example of the parents and other elders is, of course, a most important factor in habituating boys and girls to their respective roles, but their reading also plays a considerable part in the process. Very often, one imagines, the boy who interests himself in poetry, or the girl who reads about locomotives, risks disparagement on the part of elders and contemporaries, and, what is more, the book adds its own authority to this disapproval when, as is often the case, it is obviously intended for the opposite sex. Writers of children's books, that is to say, do a great deal, deliberately and otherwise, to transmit to their readers modes of feeling, thought and action, deemed by society to be appropriate to their age and sex.

The taste for non-fiction, however acquired, is stronger among the boys than among the girls. At no age does it form more than ten per cent of all the books borrowed by the girls, whereas roughly a quarter of all those borrowed by the boys aged ten are works of information, and the proportion is relatively high at every age.

Children are given a good deal of encouragement, at school and elsewhere, to read such books, often at the expense of fiction, supposedly more frivolous and less educative. It may be a mistake, however, to urge children to devote much time to reading for information at the stage when it is vital that they should learn to read effortlessly and with enjoyment. Works of information are generally longer and more difficult to read than works of fiction, and the child who reads non-fiction is likely to read fewer books in total. In support of this it may be observed that the amount of borrowing at each age tends to vary inversely with the amount of non-fiction taken out.[1] Among the boys aged ten, for example, when the amount of non-fiction read is at its highest, the total number of books borrowed is lower than at almost any age. Even more serious, perhaps, is the fact that as the amount of non-fiction rises the variety of all books borrowed tends to be more restricted. There is at least a suspicion that when children are encouraged at too early an age to read for information they may fail to read books in sufficient numbers to ensure that they gain the fluency in reading and the catholicity of taste which will enable them to derive continued pleasure from books.

In this respect, the reading habits of the girls appear generally healthier than the boys'. From year to year the girls' reading increases in variety and amount, whereas among the boys the number of books borrowed tends if anything to decline with age, and their variety to become more limited. The fact that the boys are more addicted to non-fiction than are the girls may have a bearing on this question. Moreover, the records of individual readers tend to confirm the impression that those who borrow only works of information are seldom avid readers. Among the readers who borrowed no fiction at all, the one who borrowed most—a boy aged ten—took out only nine books in the year, while many others visited the Library only

---

[1]Figure 5

once or twice. At the other end of the scale stands the ten-year-old girl who read little else but fiction, and who took out 165 books in the year. There can be little doubt that she is more likely than the boys to develop an interest in reading which will endure into later life, if only because she has had more opportunity to acquire fluency in reading, and to experience the wide variety of the benefits and satisfactions which books afford.

While, undeniably, there is value to children in reading books which add to their knowledge or their skill, even more important, it may be, are books which minister to their spiritual and moral development. "Most boys and girls", says the Newsom Report,[1] "want to be what they call 'being good' and they want to know what this really implies in the personal situations which confront them. They also want to know what kind of animal a man is, and whether ultimately each one of them matters—and, if so, why and to whom". Many adults look to literature for the answers to these questions, and it is evident from the books they read at different stages that children, too, consciously or unconsciously, look to stories for guidance in growing up. A balanced programme of reading during these formative years must include not only works of information, but also many which the child may read with little effort and for mere enjoyment. Though these may appear to have less immediate value, through reading them the child develops facility for reading and a growing appetite for books. If, in addition, they sharpen the child's awareness of himself and of other human beings, the total benefit they confer is very great.

---

[1]Ministry of Education : Central Advisory Council for Education : *Half our Future*, H.M.S.O. 1963, p. 52.

CHAPTER III

FROM EASY BOOKS TO DIFFICULT

IT is obvious that children are swayed in their choice of books by considerations other than of mere subject-matter. Between two Fairy or two Adventure stories there may be many differences which serve to make one more attractive than the other, some of them differences in physical make-up—size, print and illustrations, others related to the content—language, style and treatment.

While there is no denying that a well-produced book appeals to children of all ages, it is only for the very young that the external appearance of a book is important in its own right. To the infant unaware of the distinction between books and playthings, the colour, size and shape may be the attributes which make a book attractive, but to slightly older children the physical appearance of a book is important principally because it enables them to judge the suitability of the contents. Illustrations, for example, are all too often ill-produced and unattractive in themselves, but this is of no great relevance to the slower reader, whose main concern is that they should show him quickly whether the book is of the kind he likes, and that they should supplement his understanding of the text. Apart from knowing what the book is about, before he makes his choice the reader needs to know whether it is within reach of his understanding and his capacity to read. The shape of the book, the number of pages, the amount of illustration and the size of print are important because they enable him to come to a decision on this question.

Format

Today, the very size of the page often distinguishes the book intended for the very young. The great majority of adult books are produced in Octavo format of Large Foolscap, Crown, Large Post or Demy papers. The resulting pages range in size from approximately $6\frac{1}{2}$ by $4\frac{1}{2}$ inches to $9\frac{1}{2}$ by $6\frac{1}{2}$ inches, while pages smaller or larger than this are nowadays mainly associated with young children's books. This has not always been the case. In 1623 Shakespeare's plays appeared in a Folio volume, and before that they had been published in Quarto editions. Late in the eighteenth century, very small books in Duo-decimo were much in vogue, while towards the end of the nineteenth, books with large pages and wide margins became very popular. In modern times, however, for reasons no doubt connected with the economics of mass production, the medium-sized Octavo format has become virtually standard for adult books, other formats being reserved principally for books not enjoying a wide sale and for those intended for the very young.

It may well be that young children prefer very small books for the good reason that they are more convenient to their small hands, and very large books because they lie easily across their knees, but more important is the fact that very small and very large pages have through usage become associated in their minds with books for the very young. The result is, as Table 1 shows, that as they grow older children tend increasingly to choose books with pages in Octavo size.

	Boys	Girls
Age 6	48	40
7	48	51
8	69	64
9	83	64
10	84	92
11	90	91
12	90	94

TABLE 1. Books in Octavo Format, as a percentage of total issues to each age group.

Among readers at the age of six, less than half the books borrowed are in this format, the remainder being divided roughly equally between the very large and the very small. Nor, at this age, are the books chosen all of the familiar shape ; many are wider than they are long, others very long and very narrow. Readers become more conservative in their choice of format as they grow. Books in unusual shapes and sizes fall sharply out of favour when children reach the age of eight, and by the age of twelve, 90 per cent or more of the books they choose are similar in format to adult books.

The format of a book tends therefore to be regarded as one indi-cation of the age-group for which it is intended, and it is at least possible that children are sometimes put off taking out a book simply because its appearance has given them a wrong impression, or even because they are anxious lest others who might see them read it should form a wrong impression. It is true that the ten-year-old boys take out an unusually large number of big books, most of them works of information ; even so, it seems likely that the custom of producing works of information and books of poetry in unusual shapes and sizes does little to enhance their popularity with older children. At the same time, older children who are backward in reading are undoubtedly discouraged from borrowing books which are within their grasp, because their format makes it obvious that they are intended for younger children. In order to preserve their self-esteem, backward readers need books which, in external appearance at least, are indistinguishable from those borrowed by their abler age-mates.

Number of Pages

The thickness of a book—the number of pages it contains—provides the reader with another indication of its suitability. One might expect that, as children become more fluent in their reading, they would in general choose longer books. The median length of the books borrowed from the Library rises from approximately fifty pages at the age of six to two hundred pages at the age of twelve. That is to say, one half of the books issued to the six-year-olds contain more than fifty pages, and one half of the books borrowed by the twelve-year-olds contain more than two-hundred pages. Progress towards longer books is slow between the ages of six and seven, while children are mastering the mechanics of reading in their first year at the junior school, but thereafter quickly gains momentum. By the age of nine, the girls are borrowing books one-half of which contain at least 150 pages, while the boys by this stage have made even better progress and are borrowing books with a median length of 190 pages. The boys' apparent superiority at this point is explained by the fact that a relatively high proportion of the books they borrow consists of works of information which are commonly very long. On the other hand, of course, they borrow at this age an average of only thirteen books a year, little more than half the number borrowed by the girls. On balance, therefore, at this age as at every age after that of eight, in terms of total quantity of reading the girls are in the lead.

Age	Boys		Girls			
	(a) Mean number of Pages	(b) Standard Deviation	(c) Mean number of Pages	(d) Standard Deviation	(e) Difference (a)—(c)	(f) Standard Error of Difference
6	72	32	62	44	10	3.2*
7	87	66	76	51	11	4.1*
8	138	74	101	59	37	4.2**
9	179	66	150	64	29	3.3**
10	180	62	173	59	7	2.9
11	196	54	183	61	13	2.8**
12	210	51	205	55	5	2.9

    *   Differences Significant at 1% level.

   **   Differences Significant at .1% level.

TABLE 2.   Analysis of issues to each age group, showing average number of pages per book.

Beyond the age of nine, the average length of the books rises more slowly as, after the first rapid steps towards mastery of reading, progress becomes more gradual. Even so, there are wide differences between individuals of the same age. Occasionally, a twelve-year-old may pick a book containing only twenty pages, while at the other extreme another may choose one more than three hundred pages long. It is not unusual to find the same range of variation among the books borrowed by a single reader, but by and large the majority of the books taken out by any reader tend to fall within a narrower bracket, and the more advanced readers can be distinguished from the more retarded to some extent on the basis of the number of pages in the books they customarily choose. The books issued to the twelve-year-olds tend to show more uniformity of length than do those issued to those aged eleven or less, mainly because fairly suddenly at this point children stop borrowing books with fewer than, say, 120 pages. This, one suspects, is not due to any sudden increase in reading ability ; by this time many children have stopped borrowing from the Library, the majority of these, of course, being children whose reading ability is low. It is evident that twelve-year-olds will continue to read only if they are able to enjoy the books appropriate to their age, and to do so they need to be accustomed to reading books of reasonable length, perhaps between 170 and 230 pages long.

Illustrations

The shortest books of all are generally picture books, in which at least one half of all the pages are given up to full-page coloured illustrations. More than half those borrowed by the six-year-olds are of this kind, but beyond the age of seven as reading skills improve they fall rapidly out of favour. Nevertheless, pictures continue to hold a prominent place in the books which children borrow. Full-page illustrations for which the printed word merely provides captions give way to smaller pictures inserted in, and subordinate to, the text, but in the books issued to the eight-year-olds pictures take up roughly one-fifth of the total space, and in those borrowed by the twelve-year-olds, still occupy about four per cent. For the younger and less skilful readers, pictures are essential to their understanding of the book, and in works of information—in technical books and encyclopedias— they perform the same service for even older readers. In the fiction read by the older children they gradually come to have a different function. The full-page coloured frontispiece often found in the book intended for the eleven- or twelve-year-old serves to give the would-be reader some indication of the contents by which to judge its suitability ; the small black-and-white illustrations in the text, when not purely decorative, tend to convey the mood and atmosphere of the story rather than specific situations or events.

	Boys	Girls
Age 6	51	53
7	50	48
8	18	27
9	6	15
10	7	8
11	6	6
12	4	4

TABLE 3. Percentage of pages given to illustration. The figures give the median percentage for each age group.

Between books in which the burden of meaning is borne almost entirely by the pictures and those in which pictures are sparse and inessential come those, borrowed chiefly by the eight- and nine-year-olds, in which illustrations, usually in black and white, have a prominent though subordinate place, and punctuate the printed text at intervals with a visual summary of the situation. The extent to which readers rely upon these pictures varies, no doubt, with their reading skill, but their presence in a book ensures that its meaning can be understood by children of widely different ability. The popularity Enid Blyton's books enjoy among children of different ages and levels of achievement is in part explained by the fact that, while for the abler readers the printed text is sufficient in itself, others are given substantial help by the frequent illustrations. It seems unfortunate that very few books which, in content, are suitable for older children, make use of illustrations in this way. It is worth considering whether many of the slower readers might not persist a little longer—long enough perhaps to acquire the reading habit—if in the sort of books they could enjoy there were sufficient illustrations to supplement their understanding of the print.

Size of Type

Not only the illustrations but the quality of the print itself can help to ease the slower reader's difficulties. That of Burt (1959) is the most recent of many studies of the effects of different kinds of print upon readability. The size, design and boldness of the type, the length of line, width of margins, interlinear spacing, all interact with one another to render print legible or otherwise, but, Burt concludes, the main factors which decide whether print is suitable for readers of a given age are the size of type and the interlinear spacing. When learning to read, children usually proceed from word to word, or even from letter to letter, and at this stage large type and wide spacing are most suitable because they facilitate recognition of these small units. To fluent readers, on the other hand, reading is essentially a process of assimilating groups of words in sequences long enough to convey meaning. For them, therefore, it is important that print, while large enough to permit words and letters to be identified, should yet be small enough to allow a fair number of words to be encompassed within the visual span. Children, and especially older children, therefore find print that is too large just as difficult to read as print

Age yrs.	Boys		Girls		(e) Difference (d)—(a)	(f) Standard Error of Difference
	(a) Mean Size of Type	(b) Standard Deviation	(c) Mean Size of Type	(d) Standard Deviation		
6	18.70	4.70	19.54	4.95	1.14	.41*
7	19.10	4.95	19.70	4.66	.60	.33
8	15.46	3.50	17.05	4.54	1.51	.28**
9	13.56	2.83	14.98	3.48	1.42	.17**
10	13.31	2.21	13.74	2.73	.43	.01**
11	12.89	1.77	13.20	2.58	.31	.03**
12	12.65	1.39	12.84	1.59	.29	.08**

    *   Differences significant at 1% level.
    **   Differences significant at .1% level.

TABLE 4. Analysis of issues to each age group, showing mean size of type, in points. (1 Point = 1/72 ins.).

that is too small. Thus, according to Burt, children under seven find it easiest to read print which has twelve lines to five inches of page, while children over twelve find least difficulty with print which has thirty lines to five inches.[1]

It is customary to measure type in ' points,' a point being 0.013837", or approximately one seventy-second of an inch. The ' body ' of a type is the measure in points of the height of the block upon which the type is cast. It is therefore equivalent to the height of the printed letter plus the space separating the letter from the line below. The print found by Burt to be most suitable for those under seven is equivalent therefore to type of thirty points, while twelve point type is most suited to those over twelve years of age. Type of the latter size is commonly employed in adult books.

After measuring the print in the books borrowed by children at each age, it was obvious that they tend to choose books which conform fairly closely to the standards Burt found to be appropriate to their

[1]Op. cit., p. 12.

age. One half of the books issued to borrowers aged six are printed in type of twenty points or more, while the median size of type in books selected by the twelve-year-olds is approximately thirteen points. Table 4 shows clearly how children tend, as they grow older, to read books with smaller print.

The preference these children show at the age of eight or nine for more closely printed books is certainly the outcome of the rapid improvement in reading skills which follows entry to the junior school. Type of 17 points or more still predominates, however, in the books picked by the girls at eight years of age, when the boys have already graduated to print of less than fifteen points. In later years, too, the boys tend to select somewhat smaller print than do the girls. To some extent this reflects their greater liking for informative books, which are often set in quite small type. There is the other possibility, however, that boys whose reading ability is low are less prone than the girls to borrow from the Library. At the age of eleven, for instance, girls occasionally borrow books with print as large as thirty points or more ; at this age no boy borrowed a book of more than twenty-one points. From about the age of nine, compared with girls, relatively few of the boys who join the Library borrow books with large type. This suggests that those boys who by this time are unable to read fairly small print with ease are unlikely to be attracted to the Library.

Reading Ease

The size of the print is, of course, but one of the factors which go to determine the readability of a text. More important, certainly, is the difficulty or otherwise of the language for which the print is a vehicle, and it is not surprising that Whitehead (1956) should have found that when choosing fiction children look for simple language.

It is not an easy matter to decide what makes one piece of writing more intelligible to the reader than another. Stolurov and Newman (1959) consider that no fewer than twenty-three factors may inter-act to determine whether a passage of prose will be easy or difficult to read, and of these a predominance of monosyllabic words and short sentences are the main characteristics making for easy reading. In order to measure readability, various formulae have been devised, notably by Lorge (1944) and Flesch (1948). The former takes into account not only vocabulary and sentence length but certain aspects of syntax and sentence structure ; the latter, which is based solely on the average number of syllables per word and of words per sentence, is more easy to apply, especially when the tables compiled by Farr and Jenkins (1949) are employed. A score of 100 on the Flesch Readability scale indicates language made up almost entirely of monosyllabic words arranged in sentences averaging nine words or so in length. Language as easy as this is found only in the simplest children's books and can be understood by readers possessing very elementary skill. At the other extreme, scores of twenty or less indicate very difficult or technical language, intelligible only to very skilful readers or to those familiar with the subject-matter. Between these extremes, the language of children's comics scores 90 points or more, pulp fiction 80, digests and popular non-fiction 60.[1]

As Carsley (1957) points out,[2] and as was evident from observation of members of the Library, before choosing a book children almost invariably sample some of it, usually the opening paragraphs, partly perhaps to assure themselves that they have not read it before, and partly to find out if it can be read with reasonable ease. In order to discover the kind of language children look for in the books they choose, the Flesch Readability formula was applied to the first hundred words of every book issued to members, with the exception of those which were issued only once in the year. The resulting score is not a reliable measure of the difficulty of the entire book, since the style of the opening paragraph is not always typical of the rest, but for the present purpose we are not so much concerned with its actual readability as with the impression given to the child who samples the first paragraph or two.

As is shown in Table 5, younger readers tend to look for easy books, and older children are prepared to accept more difficult ones. The median score in those borrowed at the age of six is 83, falling by the age of twelve to 70 among those borrowed by the boys, to 74 among those issued to the girls. What is more surprising is the fact that

---

[1]Flesch, R. ; op. cit.

Michaelis and Tyler (1951) found language scoring between 20 and 30 intelligible to college graduates ; between 30 and 40 intelligible to college undergraduates ; 45 to Grade XIII students.

Sward and Harris (1952) found that between 1873 and 1945, the readability score of certain American magazines for children remained fairly constant between 75 and 85.

[2]Op. cit., page 21.

Age yrs.	Boys		Girls		(e) Difference $(c)-(a)$	(f) Standard Error of Difference
	(a) Mean Reading Ease Score	(b) Standard Deviation	(c) Mean Reading Ease Score	(d) Standard Deviation		
6	83.5	9.99	82.3	10.20	−1.2	.86
7	82.0	10.74	82.0	10.16		
8	76.3	12.33	80.5	10.45	4.2	.73**
9	71.4	13.70	79.3	12.70	7.9	.71**
10	72.3	13.21	78.0	11.40	5.7	.63**
11	75.1	12.96	77.2	11.70	2.1	.53**
12	70.2	12.65	73.7	12.91	3.5	.71**

** Differences significant at .1% level.

TABLE 5. Analysis of issues, showing mean scores for Reading Ease.

progress, as is evident from these figures, is so very slow, especially among the girls. Even the oldest children tend to avoid books which promise to be at all difficult to read ; of those borrowed by the twelve-year-olds, no more than 15 per cent have scores of less than 60, the remainder being all easier to read than popular digests. Boys of the age of nine or ten, it is true, seem a little more prepared than others to tolerate some difficulty in their books, doubtless because at that stage they have considerable interest in works of information. When this phase passes at the age of eleven, the boys, like the girls, obviously prefer, in the fiction which they read, language which presents no obstacles to their swift following of the narrative.

There is evidence from other quarters that the books which children find enjoyable are rarely difficult enough to put a strain upon their reading skill. McDonald (1953), for example, found considerable discrepancies between the reading ability of secondary modern school children and the demands made on them by the books they most preferred. Hugh Lofting's *Doctor Doolittle*, for instance, though its readability score suggested that it was suitable for nine-year-olds, proved most popular among the twelve-year-olds, and in the majority of other instances, McDonald found a difference of at least one year between what he terms a book's popularity age and its readability age.[1] He also makes the suggestion that boys are more prone than girls to read books appropriate to their ability, and this is borne out by the present evidence that except at the ages of six and seven the boys borrow books which are in general more difficult than those borrowed by the girls. This is perhaps another indication that the weaker readers among the boys tend not to join the Library.

Simplicity of language is but one of the qualities which distinguish the style of one book from that of another. Flesch has pointed out[2] that the language of, say, a scientific treatise differs from that of a personal anecdote in the incidence of colloquialisms, abbreviations, dialogue, proper nouns, and pronouns referring to individuals. The extent to which these elements are found in reading matter is a measure of what Flesch terms its human interest. On the scale devised by Flesch for measuring human interest, reading material is classified as Dramatic (Score 60—100), Highly Interesting (40—60), Interesting (20—40), Mildly Interesting (10—20) or Dull (0—10). Flesch claims, probably with reason, that language which has a high degree of human interest is more easily comprehended by the reader, and insists that the human interest of a text be taken into account as well as its reading ease in order to assess its readability.

Flesch's formula for calculating human interest was applied to the first one hundred words of each book issued, again excepting those which had been issued only once. This confirmed, if confirmation is necessary, that children look for a high degree of human interest in their books. The girls especially showed a strong preference for books written in what Flesch describes as a dramatic style : at least one-half of the books they borrowed at each age scored more than 60 on the scale of human interest. The median score of the books chosen by the boys fell somewhat below this at the ages of eight, nine, ten, and twelve, reaching its lowest point of 48 at the age of ten. This reflects the relative popularity among boys at certain ages of works of information, in which, naturally, the style is far less racy and colloquial than is general in works of fiction. In terms of human interest, the contrast between the books chosen by the boys and those chosen by the girls is sharpest at the age of ten when the boys' fondness for non-fiction is at its height. For reasons which are not immediately apparent, the boys

---

[1]Op. cit., p. 45.
[2]Op. cit.

at the age of eleven borrow more books in total than at the age of ten, but proportionately fewer works of information. Whereas at the age of ten the boys' reading is much more 'serious' than the girls', the difference is much smaller at the age of eleven.

	Boys	Girls
Age 6	62	63
7	62	61
8	54	61
9	51	67
10	48	68
11	62	67
12	54	63

TABLE 6. Analysis of issues to each age group, showing median scores for Human Interest.

It would be possible, from the fore-going data, to construct a profile, so to speak, of the superficial features—format, length, print, illustrations, style—of the average book that appeals to the average boy or girl at a given age. This might even have some value as a guide to those concerned with the selection and provision of books suitable for children, but it might imply much more uniformity of taste than in fact occurs. Far more important, at least to the teacher, than the task of catering for what are imagined to be the average tastes of the class is that of ensuring that each child reads at his or her own level, and makes the best progress he or she is capable of towards more mature reading. Side by side with the business of giving the requisite training in the basic reading skills should go that of guiding children to books which will help them to develop the fluency which is essential to enjoyment. The sheer volume of reading is decisive here, and it is vitally important that the books which children are encouraged to read for pleasure are not so difficult as to hinder rapid reading. We have seen that, when free to choose for themselves, children usually read books which are well within their capacity, and that, at least in language, the books chosen by the twelve-year-olds are not vastly more difficult than those picked by children of six or seven. This, perhaps, affords a clue to the treatment of the slower reader. Through careful selection, it should often prove possible to give the slower reader the satisfying experience of reading books which are not patently less demanding than those read by other children. Certainly he will find neither pride nor pleasure in reading books obviously intended for readers much younger than himself. On the other hand, he might find it possible to read books containing quite as many pages, and on subjects much the same as in those enjoyed by others of his age, if the print were slightly larger, the illustrations more numerous and more informative, the sentences slightly shorter, and the style a little more dramatic. Nor would the better readers necessarily be repelled by such a book ; among the books of Enid Blyton there are many which, by virtue of their large type, frequent illustrations, simple language and colloquial style, are within the scope of quite young children, and yet retain their popularity with older readers.

The time given to reading instruction in our schools is justifiable only if the children thereafter make full and proper use of the skill they have acquired. There is good reason to believe that unless the reading habit is deeply ingrained when they are at school, many children will allow their skill to fall into disuse once they leave. Enquiries among National Service men[1] have revealed that many of those who had made some use of libraries while at school no longer did so two years later. Even among those leaving grammar schools, the proportion using libraries fell from 89 to 55 per cent, while among secondary modern pupils the decline was even steeper, from 68 to 16 per cent. For many boys, we suggest, the moment of decision comes at about the age of eleven or twelve, at the end of their primary school lives, or very early in their secondary school careers. It is of particular importance at this stage that everything possible should be done to sustain their interest in reading. A renewed effort may be necessary at this time to perfect the reader's skills to the point of enabling him to read with pleasure the kinds of books appropriate to his new status, both as a student entering upon the secondary phase of education, and as a human being trying to meet the changes, within himself and without, which accompany adolescence. More is implied than a remedial course for backward readers ; what is intended rather is that reading instruction for the majority of children should move into a second phase in which the emphasis is upon increasing the speed and fluency of reading by means of techniques evolved for this purpose

[1]Central Advisory Council for Education ; (1959), "15 to 18".

in recent years and fairly commonly employed in American schools and colleges.

The quality of reading instruction given in schools is not to be measured by the mere quantity of printed matter consumed ; nevertheless, sheer voracity on the part of the young reader is the surest means of gaining fluency and of strengthening the reading habit, and constitutes the prerequisite of continued progress towards mature reading tastes. This emphasises the importance of making available to children a plentiful supply of books so graded in respect of readability that the learner's confidence never falters, and his pleasure in reading is never marred by fear of failure. The experiments begun in 1961, employing Pitman's Initial Teaching Alphabet, already show that the fewer obstacles there are to fluent reading, the greater are the beginner's self-confidence, his enthusiasm for reading and his interest in books.[1] The problem of maintaining this confidence and enthusiasm in later years, and especially from the age of eleven or twelve, prompts one to question whether the policy, commonly adopted by teachers of English, of encouraging the intensive study of a small number of demanding 'classics' meets the needs of the majority of children, even in our grammar schools. A programme designed to encourage extensive reading for enjoyment, especially of contemporary writings, rather than intensive study, might better serve what must be the main purpose of all literary training, that of ensuring that the learner should continue to read throughout life, and to derive pleasure and profit from his reading. To be sure, it is legitimate, even essential, to acquaint the learner with our literary tradition and our cultural heritage. The mistake is to assume that the essence of our inheritance has been crystallized for ever in certain revered writings of the past, and that to know these is essential to every educated person. The true contribution to our culture of the writers of the past, however, is surely not in their writings, but in the impression they have left indelibly on our ways of thinking, feeling and behaving. In each of the works produced today some part of that contribution is preserved ; together they embody what is of enduring value in the literature of the past. If this is true, then extensive reading of modern writings is as good a way as any other of introducing children to our common culture. But even if this were not the case, reading makes accessible to us the thoughts and

---

[1] Downing, John A. 1963. P. 23.

experiences of other men ; to sight, hearing, smell, taste and touch, it adds another sense, to be deprived of which is to be impoverished. What is above all important, then, is that children should have an insatiable appetite for books, and that means that their experience of reading should overwhelmingly be one of enjoyment, unmarred by failure or frustration.

CHAPTER IV

HEROES AND HEROINES

From a book's external features—its format, print, language and so on—a child judges how easy or difficult it will be to read, and whether, therefore, it will be within his scope of understanding. But there is more to choosing a book than that. The would-be reader looks beyond the externals to the content of the book to find whether it is to his taste. And when choosing fiction he looks especially at the central character or characters whose actions, thoughts and feelings the book recounts, for unless there is some bond of sympathy between the reader and the protagonists of the story the book must fail in its appeal.

Children tend, for reasons of which they are not necessarily aware, to look in a book for a character with whom they can identify themselves. When the reader is able to assume the identity of one of the characters, he has the illusion of participating directly in the experiences recounted in the book, and the impression made upon him is the more vivid as a result. Apart from this, an element of wish-fulfilment may be involved. Even the free-est and least frustrated of us is aware of areas of experience to which he has no access, and of satisfactions which he cannot know ; each in his own identity is subject to humiliating limitations, circumscribed in time and space, fettered to his physical frame, and subject to the pressures of the society in which he lives. All readers, therefore, irrespective of age, read partly in order to transcend their personal and temporal limitations. Children especially are prone to compensate for their own inadequacies through day-dreaming, play-acting and reading. There is another, more obviously wholesome, reason why children assume the roles of characters in fiction. They are in the process of forming their own personalities. This entails a great deal of experimentation in a variety of roles, and a great deal of imitation of many different models, the majority of which will ultimately be rejected as unsuitable or unattainable, while others are assimilated to become a permanent part of the individual's self-image. Throughout childhood and into adolescence the youngster dons a succession of different personalities, copied from the cinema, from the theatre, from books and from life, and in the process arrives at an assessment of his own limitations and potentials, and formulates his own ambitions and ideals. In this sense, therefore, the child who looks in books for characters with whom he can identify himself is performing instinctively an activity which is necessary to his development and growth.

It is rarely possible to do more than guess from which of these motives a given reader visualises himself as playing a certain role in a certain book. Sometimes, when the gap between the fictional character and the reader is very wide, as when a girl of twelve reads about a child among the fairies, or a boy of nine sees himself as a spaceman on a flight to Mars, we may suspect that the dominant desire is for escape from actuality rather than for a fuller understanding of it. Even then, however, it would be rash to assume that the desire for escape or compensation is the only motive. Why a child should wish to doff his own and don an alien personality is a matter for which no simple, clear-cut explanation can suffice.

Of course, there are many books in which there is no human being with whom the reader can identify himself. Indeed, it is rare to find a human character among the puppets in the stories read by the youngest children, and older children, at least occasionally, read books in which an animal, usually a horse or dog, plays the principal part. Moreover, throughout the years with which we are concerned, the taste continues for works of information in many of which there are no heroes or heroines of any kind. The result is that among the books chosen by boys and girls at the age of six roughly two-thirds contain no living characters at all, or have as their central figures, not human beings, but puppets, fairies, or animals.

Table 1 shows, however, that as readers grow older they increasingly demand books in which the main roles are born by human beings. Whereas in only 34 per cent of the books chosen by the boys aged six, by the age of nine in 83 per cent the centre of the stage is held by a human being. The remainder of those chosen at this age are almost entirely works of information which contain no living characters at all. The girls are rather slower to abandon stories which revolve about puppets, animals and fairies. In more than a quarter of the books they choose at the age of nine, there are still no human beings to play important parts. In later years, however, since they

	Boys (a)	Girls (b)	Difference (a)—(b)	Chi Square
	%	%		
Age 6	34	40	—6	8.7*
7	44	46	—2	
8	61	55	+6	2.8
9	83	74	+9	16.7**
10	77	88	—11	45.9**
11	88	89	—1	
12	94	97	—3	8.1*

* Significant at 1% level
** Significant at .1% level

TABLE I. Analysis of issues, showing percentage of books with human hero or heroine.

are less interested than the boys in works of information, more of their books are centred on a human being.

To consider for a moment only those books in which the focal point of interest is a human being or a group of human beings, it becomes evident that these children prefer those books in which the heroes or heroines have some resemblance to themselves. Thus the boys tend to choose stories in which the principal character is male, while the girls usually look for stories centred on a girl. There are many books, of course, which involve a group of characters of either sex, and in which boys and girls, or men and women, play equally important parts. Such books are common among those borrowed by boys and girls at every age, but among children over the age of eight they are considerably more popular with the girls than with the boys. The younger boys, as is shown in Figure 6, are moderately willing to read books intended for girls, and in which girls assume the main roles, but from about the age of nine they avoid almost entirely books which have no man or boy to play the hero. The girls are at all ages more ready to read books which are chiefly concerned with a member of the opposite sex ; indeed, until the age of eight, they are as likely to choose a book centred upon a boy as upon a girl, and although as they grow older they tend increasingly to pick books which revolve around a female character and are therefore intended exclusively for girls, even at the age of twelve they continue to read a substantial number of books ostensibly designed for boys.

Evidently the role of males in life and in society is held in some esteem by the girls, whereas the boys tend to despise the roles played by girls and women. Teachers are accustomed to bear this point in mind when selecting books for reading by mixed classes, especially beyond the age of eight or nine. More often than not, as a result, the books are chosen mainly with the boys in mind, since the girls are more accommodating in their tastes. It might be argued, however, that too exclusive a preoccupation with a world dominated by males is good neither for the boys nor for the girls. It is generally agreed that in the later years of secondary education, boys are less capable than girls of appreciating the works of the great novelists. One wonders whether a less restricted range of reading in their earlier years might not be a better preparation for the reading of adult fiction, which, after all, calls for insight into, and sympathy with, the role and character of women as well as of men. Moreover, as a preparation for mature living, there is perhaps some value in a boy's reading books which enable him to look at life through eyes other than his own or those of his own sex.

The fact is, however, that from the age of eight or nine, the boys prefer to identify themselves with male characters in fiction, the girls with females. It is curious that a boy in his reading should be able to find pleasure in assuming the identity of a Stone Age man, of a Martian, or even of a wild animal, and yet find it distasteful to adopt in imagination a female role. As a child reads a book, he tends to don the personality, or certain aspects of the personality, of one or other of its characters, as part of a continuous search for a role which is suited to his capacities and which will win for him the approval of others. It is part, as we have said, of his search for ideals, for models on which to pattern his own development. By the age of nine or so, his image of himself, though far from complete, is already taking outline ; from this time the boy tends to regard himself as irredeemably male. Other questions may remain unsettled : whether to be a scientist or an explorer, a gallant leader or a faithful follower, introvert or extravert, gregarious or solitary, conformist or rebel ; throughout his life, in fact, occasions for choosing between alternative ways of thinking, feeling and behaving will constantly arise, but on each of these questions his decision will henceforth depend in part on what he thinks befits his sex.

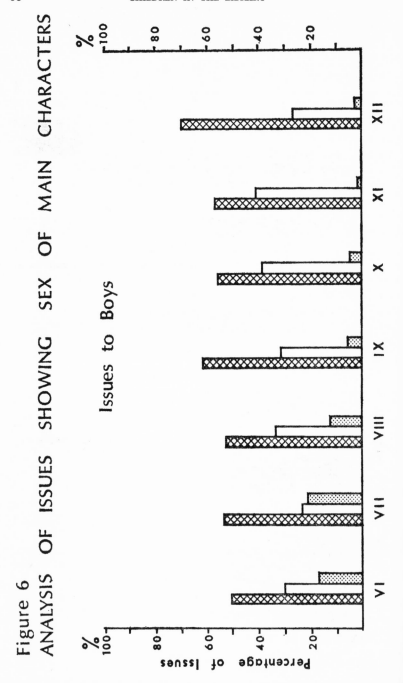

Figure 6
ANALYSIS OF ISSUES SHOWING SEX OF MAIN CHARACTERS

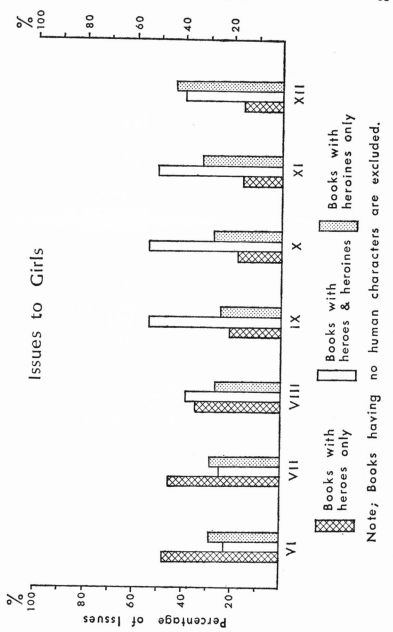

Issues to Girls

It is not enough, however, that the main character should be of the same sex as the reader ; for the most part children prefer to identify themselves with characters of approximately their own age. The books issued to the six-year-old boys may serve to illustrate this. Of the 262 books borrowed, only 87 contained a recognisable human being ; the others were all concerned with fairies, toys or animals. In 68 of the 87, the principal human character was a child of pre-school or infant school age ; in twelve, the main character was of junior school age ; in three, the hero or heroine was an adolescent, and in four an adult. Older readers, naturally, read many more books dealing with children of primary school age, and upwards, and after the age of eight very rapidly abandon stories about the very young.

It is not always easy to assign an age to the principal character. In order to render books attractive to children over a wide range of ages, authors often avoid specifying too closely the age of their characters. Others, for the same purpose, write about a group of characters of different ages, and this, too, sometimes makes it difficult to decide upon the age of the hero or heroine. Nevertheless, Figure 7 tries to show what proportion of the books borrowed at each age revolve around young children, juniors, adolescents and adults respectively. It will be seen that the majority of the heroes and heroines favoured by readers before the age of eight are themselves, so far as one can judge, below the age of seven. At the ages of eight, nine and ten, the books which the boys borrow are fairly evenly divided between those in which the main character is of primary school age and those dealing with an adolescent, but the trend is clearly towards books concerned with older characters. This is especially evident at the age of twelve, when a substantial proportion (25 per cent) of the books issued to the boys have adult heroes.

The same tendency is apparent among the girls. They, too, as they grow older tend to read stories centred upon older characters, but they lag some way behind the boys. It is noticeable, for example, that at every age fewer of their books deal with adults, and even at the age of twelve a small number of those they choose are still concerned with children less than seven years old. The differences between the boys and girls in this respect emerge more clearly, perhaps, from Table 2, which gives the average age of the main characters in the books borrowed at each age.

	Boys (a)	Girls (b)	Difference (a)—(b)	Standard Error
Age 6	5.1	5.4	—.3	.60
7	7.8	6.6	1.3	.59
8	11.0	7.8	3.3	.45**
9	13.9	9.8	4.1	.28**
10	13.7	11.1	2.6	.24**
11	13.2	12.1	1.1	.18**
12	15.0	13.0	2.0	.24**
**Significant at .1% level.				

TABLE 2. Analysis of issues, showing average age of hero or heroine.

Note : To arrive at these averages, characters of pre-school age were assumed to be aged three, junior school characters nine, adolescents fifteen, adults twenty-one.

The boys, especially after the age of seven, show a decided preference for reading about characters older than themselves. The boys of eleven are to some degree exceptional in that their books, on the whole, have younger characters than do those chosen by the boys of nine and ten. They read more books with schoolboy heroes, and fewer books with adult heroes than do younger boys, and in this sense, the boys who patronise the Library at the age of eleven seem to be less mature in their reading tastes than those who join the Library earlier. The majority of those who continue to be members at the age of twelve, however, firmly turn their backs upon stories dealing with younger children, and show an increasing preference for those with adult heroes.

In this respect, the girls seem less precocious than the boys. Although it is true that even at the ages of six and seven they read a number of books dealing with characters of primary school age or older, beyond the age of seven they are much slower than the boys in seeking books concerned with adolescents or adults. Even at the age of twelve, only rarely do they choose books with an adult hero or heroine, and it is generally the case that whereas the boys tend to identify themselves with fictional characters older than themselves, the girls more readily find themselves in sympathy with characters very close to their own age.

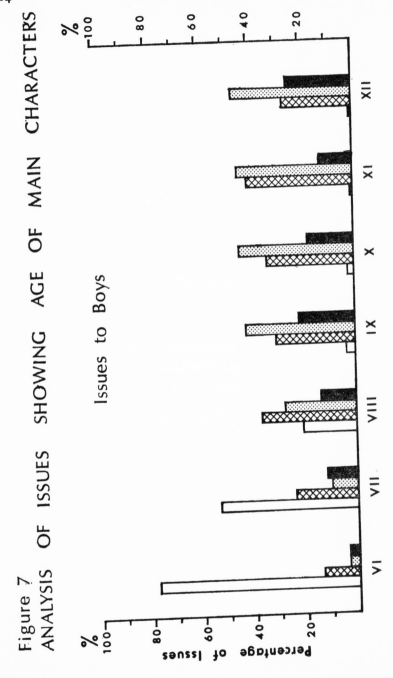

Figure 7
ANALYSIS OF ISSUES SHOWING AGE OF MAIN CHARACTERS

Issues to Boys

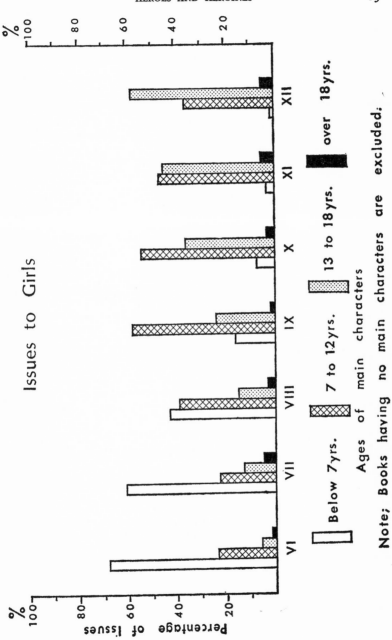

Issues to Girls

% 100 80 60 40 20

Percentage of Issues

VI VII VIII IX X XI XII

☐ Below 7yrs.   ▨ 7 to 12yrs.   ▦ 13 to 18yrs.   ■ over 18yrs.

Ages of main characters

Note; Books having no main characters are excluded.

These differences reflect two radically different attitudes to reading, the one an essentially realistic approach more common among the girls, the other an escapist approach more characteristic of the boys. There is a sense, of course, in which all reading may be said to be escapist ; the vicarious experience acquired through identification with a fictitious character cannot be equated with first-hand, actual experience. Nevertheless, there is an important difference between the reader who seeks through reading to shed light on his own immediate predicament, and one whose reading has no practical bearing on his real problems. At all events, we are justified in saying that the girls appear to read for the purposes of exploring the present, while the boys tend rather to read in order to anticipate the future.

It is usually easier for a reader to have fellow-feeling for a character of the same age and sex, but this superficial resemblance is not always essential, nor is it ever enough, to ensure that a sense of fellowship does arise. Boys and girls demand more of their heroes and heroines than that they should be of a certain age or sex ; by their qualities, their circumstances, or achievements, they must also win their readers' sympathy or admiration. Children, that is to say, look to their heroes and heroines to realise some ideal. This does not mean, at any rate for the younger readers, that the central figure must be of heroic stature ; the reader's response may well be one of sympathy rather than of admiration, but at all events, the hero or heroine must appear to the reader to be in an enviable position, and for this reason young readers almost invariably require the outcome of the story to be happy.

Children clearly envy those characters in fiction who enjoy or finally achieve a happy, stable family life. Only in Family stories does this form the central theme, but in many others of the books they choose the central figure is portrayed as being or becoming a contented, valued member of a family. In those borrowed by the younger readers it may be that a discarded doll is recovered and restored to favour, or a straying dog or pony finds a haven and a loving owner, while older readers prefer to read of waifs who find their parents, or of children who make a notable contribution to the happiness of their home.

At all ages this theme appeals much more to girls than it does to boys. At six, the differences between them in this respect are small, but from the age of seven the boys become steadily less interested in the family life of their heroes, until at the age of eleven in less than ten per cent of the books they choose is any attention given to these domestic matters. The twelve-year-olds show a little more concern with this aspect of their heroes' affairs, and this is perhaps the first sign of the development on the part of boys of an interest in emotional and psychological situations which has long characterised the girls, but which exerts a decisive influence upon the reading tastes of boys only in the period of adolescence beyond that at present being considered.

Children are also drawn to characters who enjoy or win a place as accepted and valued members of a community. In the books chosen by the younger children, animals and toys are often depicted as living together in accordance with rules and conventions which are broadly those by which human society is governed. Human values, too, prevail, and stress is often laid upon the importance of being socially accepted or admired. Approval is bestowed on characters who contribute to the general welfare or behave in accordance with acknowledged standards. Many of these stories for the very young appear to have the moral or didactic purpose, rarely openly expressed, of setting such qualities as courtesy, truthfulness and unselfishness in a favourable light. In much the same way, in many of the Gang stories read by children of junior school age, the main characters are shown living among grown-up neighbours on whose support and friendliness they can rely, or whose esteem they have gained by their qualities of character or services to the community. In Careers stories, the adolescent's desire to become a useful member of society forms the central theme, but in many books of other kinds adolescent characters are portrayed as having similar aspirations.

While this element appears in more than 20 per cent of the books borrowed by the girls at every age, it is never quite so attractive to the boys. Especially from the age of nine to that of eleven, they have scant regard for the role their heroes play as members of the community at large ; the law-abiding, the conformists, the socially acceptable, are too prosaic to win their admiration. Instead, they are more apt to choose stories in which the central character wins his place in a group of youngsters bent on activities which, if not always mischievous or directed against adults, can rarely claim to be of great advantage to society. In the stories chosen by the younger children, characters seldom belong to a gang ; more often than not, even the toys and puppets are shown as members of a family or community with a hierarchy based on age, social position or authority. It is the older readers, those aged ten, eleven and twelve especially, who expect their heroes and heroines to justify themselves among their age-mates and to give their first allegiance to the gang rather than to the family or community. This is the period during which the School story, the Pony story and the Gang story are at the height of their popularity, but in many others of the books read at this time a great deal of stress is laid upon the importance of having friends and being popular. Typical of these are the Mystery stories of Enid Blyton which owe their overwhelming popularity over other tales of mystery largely to the fact that they offer their readers vicarious membership of a peer group.

As the Adventure story grows in favour, especially with boys, a new kind of hero comes to the fore, usually an adolescent but one whose achievements win for him admittance to an exclusive circle of adult males. In the Western stories of Rex Dixon, for example, the lad Pocomoto wins his spurs as a member of a cowboy band, while in the stories of Percy F. Westerman another youth is shown winning his place in a ship's crew. An even more illuminating instance is that of the sixteen-year-old boy who, in the stories of Eric Leyland, is as trusty and aggressive as any of the followers of Rip Randall, and who first wins his place in this band of fighters against crime by dint of having been expelled from school for nearly shooting the headmaster with a .22 rifle. These characters inhabit a world from which females are excluded ; their allegiance is neither to the family, to their peers, nor to society at large, but solely to the male band, to which the youth is admitted on giving evidence of remarkable virility. In much the same way, in the stories of Elsie J. Oxenham, girls are admitted to a select company of their elders by virtue of their femininity, evidenced by their having been May Queens, or being adept at certain esoteric dances.

From the age of nine, boys are increasingly attracted to books having heroes of this kind, and by the age of twelve no less than a quarter of the books they choose are of this type. Among the girls, too, it is the older ones who mostly read these stories, but it is to be remembered that, apart from those of Elsie J. Oxenham, few books intended for girls have heroines of this sort. When girls are interested in the kind of story which represents adult life in these romantic terms, in which grown-ups are portrayed as a species apart, immune to social pressures, contemptuous of convention, authority and civic obligation, they have to make do, for the most part, with Adventure stories intended principally for boys.

In any case, girls are much less addicted to these stories than are boys, being much more inclined to read of characters whose prestige is due to their position in the family, community or peer group. They are no less concerned than boys with the prospect of achieving adult status, but they envisage it in much more realistic terms. Through day-long contact with the mother in the home, they are familiar with the role of adult women in real life. They learn sufficient of the truth about women's position and activities to be able to reject flagrantly distorted versions in their fiction. Boys on the other hand have fewer opportunities to observe the father's daily life, and there are fewer checks upon the fantasies they weave about the world of men. It is a world from which they are excluded, and it therefore exerts on them the fascination of the secret and forbidden ; their imagination invests it with mystery and peril, and the men who move in it with superhuman qualities and powers. Not unexpectedly, then, older boys seek to identify themselves with youths who have been initiated into this world, or with characters of heroic stature, at a time when girls attach themselves to adolescent heroines who gain some standing in the every-day world, and who win the respect of older men and women by virtue of common-place human qualities and talents.

The main characters in the books read by the very young are portrayed differently in certain other ways from those in the books enjoyed by older children. In the former, the child, animal or toy occupying the main role is generally described in very simple terms as embodying perhaps a single trait of character—curiosity, friendliness or mischief. In contrast, the main figures in books enjoyed by older readers are more complex ; they are depicted in a wider range of circumstances and reveal more facets of their personality. Not only that, but the capabilities with which they are endowed are different. It goes almost without saying that the attributes a young boy looks for in his heroes are not always highly regarded by older readers, or by readers of the opposite sex. To find an illustration of this, one might look at books in which the main character is depicted as in need of care and protection, as being dependent for his well-being upon older and stronger members of the family or community. The children who read these books, it may be supposed, are greatly concerned with their own need for affection and security, and are therefore disposed to envy characters who in stories succeed in eliciting protective responses from those around. Stories centred upon such characters form roughly a quarter of all the books read by the boys before the age of eight, and by the girls before the age of nine. Naturally, as they grow older, readers find themselves less in sympathy with characters in this submissive role, though they continue to appear relatively often in the books which girls select.

In our society, the child draws upon many sources for an image of the role deemed suitable for him or her to play, but enough has been said to show how influential is the contribution made by books. They undoubtedly play a part in bringing about the acceptance by boys and girls of the idea that submissiveness and dependence are to be admired in the female and despised in the male. Their reading confirms them, too, in the view that it becomes a girl to be self-effacing, sympathetic, obedient and affectionate, and that to be self-assertive, unemotional, rebellious and aggressive is fitting in a boy. Look, for example, at the contrast of attitudes between boys and girls towards animals in fiction. Boys and girls alike enjoy reading stories in which characters display their control over an animal, especially a horse, but to compare the Cowboy stories which the boys enjoy with the Pony stories popular among the girls is to see that for the former the possession of a horse expresses the urge to dominate and excel, for the latter the need to love and be loved. Significantly, it is only the younger boys who read Cowboy stories ; as they grow older they turn to books in which the hero shows his mastery over machines.

This aptly illustrates a vital principle concerning the relationship between the reader and the book. It is in keeping with what we know of the selective nature of the processes of perception and retention that each reader should, so to speak, re-write for himself each book he reads, extracting from it, or even if need be adding to it, according to his own requirements. It is not necessary to suppose that the boy who enjoys Cowboy stories is fond of horses or wishes to become a cowboy ; all we can safely say is that for him the cowboy and the horse are apt symbols of important personal needs and aspirations, and that what these are is seldom immediately apparent. We cannot say what inner meaning a book may hold for a given reader, nor that its inner meaning will be the same for every child. On the contrary, we may be sure that for each reader the book will serve as a metaphor which each will interpret for himself.

What is common to most children, however, is the ambition to grow up, and this preoccupation strongly influences their choice of reading matter, and is reflected clearly in their liking for books about characters rather older than themselves. There is no blue-print with the child which dictates how he must grow. Human beings have within themselves the capacity to develop in a wide variety of ways, to become primitive savages proudly hunting heads, or Christian gentlemen delighting in good works. Essential to the process of growing up is the task of discovering the range of possible identities permitted to us, and of choosing our own identity within that range. Children take pleasure in endless questioning, in imitating, in play-acting, in day-dreaming and in reading—all of them activities which in one way or another help them to find answers to two insistent questions: What is it like to be a human being? What sort of human being shall I be?

The folk-tales current among different tribes of American Indians have been shown to advertise the traits of personality honoured in respective cultures.[1] The early training of a Navajo child, for instance, lays stress upon independence, self-assertion and competitive achievement, and Navajo folk-tales reflect the social value placed upon these attributes. In contrast, the traditional stories of the Flatheads lay little stress upon these qualities, which their easy-going mode of living and their indulgent methods of child-rearing do nothing to encourage. Like these primitive folk-tales, modern children's stories uphold values which are sanctioned by the culture from which they spring, and like them play a part in disseminating the standards current in the society to which their audiences belong. As befits the complexity of our society, however, the code postulated in children's books is far less unified and self-consistent than that expounded in the lore of a primitive tribe. Specialisation and differentiation of functions according to age, sex, class, occupation and the like, have led to the formulation in our society of a variety of codes, often mutually contradictory, but each relevant to one or other of the many roles the individual may be called upon to fill. If one common precept does emerge from the many principles of conduct severally urged by all these children's books, it is the importance of being acceptable to a group, whether it

---

[1]McClelland, David C., and Friedman, G. A. 1952.

be the family, the gang, or the community, and of shaping one's attitudes and conduct to ensure one's acceptance.

Though its author may not intend it to be such, a book for children is in a sense a parable prescribing certain attitudes, values and actions as means to the achieving of certain goals. These goals are seen in terms of status, as positions of prestige in a given social context. The story has a happy ending : the hero's right to the status he desires is confirmed, and the role he plays in order to achieve this end is vindicated. Like the folk-tale in primitive societies, the modern children's story gives public sanction to certain aims and motivations, and sets a seal on certain means to their fulfilment. For this reason, the books he reads are powerful among the influences which go to shape the child's conception of his goals and of the adjustments he must make in order to attain them. As he grows, the child's idea of his own potentialities and purposes undergoes inevitable change, which his reading itself may help to bring about. His changing ideals are reflected in his reading tastes. In his progress towards maturity, self-understanding, and a fuller and more realistic appraisal of his place and functions in the world, the heroes to whom he gives allegiance are successively more mature and more obviously human in their motives and their pattern of behaviour. The centre of the stage is occupied in turn by the child whose amiability wins recognition in the home, the boy or girl whose loyalty and boldness are valued by their companions, the youngster whose qualities find favour with grown-ups of the same sex, and finally the adolescent or adult accorded a full place in the community at large.

The reader picks a book in which the hero plays a role to which he himself aspires. More often than not, the hero is older than the reader himself, and achieves a higher status than he himself has yet gained. By identifying himself with such a figure, the reader acquires vicarious experience of a role which he anticipates his coming life will call on him to play. His reading is an imaginative rehearsal of his future adaptations. Each of the books he chooses presents him with a model for his imitation ; he accepts the model as appropriate if the status and achievement which it promises are such as he himself would like to claim, and therefore he will tend to select books which crystallise this image of his ideal self until developments in his external life render it inadequate or obsolete. He gives his admiration to the hero who in fiction successfully overcomes the obstacles which frustrate his own development in real life, and in his hero's consistent triumph over difficulties he looks for clues to his own unresolved problems. His chosen heroes therefore provide us with an index to the reader's emotional maturity : too protracted an interest in heroes of one kind would lead us to suspect that some serious obstacle is hindering his emotional development, and in such an instance it might afford us some insight into the nature of his problem to look at the kinds of difficulties with which his heroes are continually wrestling. Prolonged frustration in real life may well induce the reader to regress to forms of reading more appropriate to children younger than himself, and to substitute for the satisfactions denied him in reality the satisfaction of identifying himself with a successful character in fiction.

In any case, there is a certain ambivalence in the reader's attitude towards the hero he professedly admires. To admire a real person might entail an acceptance of his own inferiority ; to admire a fictitious character involves no such self-abasement. The pleasure he derives from sharing in a fictitious hero's triumph is all the keener because he knows himself to be real, and therefore superior to the fictional creation. Undoubtedly, this awareness of their superiority enhances the pleasure which young children have in following the exploits of animals and toys. In many of the books selected by the boys aged six, as we have seen, there is no human character with whom the reader can identify himself. This is not to say that he does not see himself in the role played by the animal or toy ; on the contrary, he does so the more readily because he knows himself superior to the creatures in the book, and less vulnerable than they. It has been suggested[1] that children who are afraid of some object often like that object more than any other when it is presented in miniature form or as a toy, and that by means of these symbols they can sometimes overcome difficulties that are otherwise beyond control. In much the same way, through his reading the child fortifies himself against fear, failure and inadequacy, by taking to himself the triumphs of a being demonstrably inferior to himself. The boys by the age of nine, and the girls a little after, are able to dispense with the more patently unreal of these devices. Thereafter the chief characters in the books they choose are almost always human beings, but although the figures are no longer so obviously puppets, these older readers find no difficulty in distinguish-

---

[1]Griffiths, D. C. (1932) P. 164.

ing between them and real people. The capacity to make this distinction is necessary for the reader's enjoyment of stories. It enables him at will to identify himself with, or dissociate himself from, the character presented in the story. This is most necessary, perhaps, when the fictional being is involved in situations intolerable to the reader in his own identity. For this reason, when the younger readers choose a book in which the main character is faced with serious hazards—with being lost, kidnapped, or injured—the book is almost always one in which the character so threatened is a puppet figure. On the other hand, even the youngest readers are prepared to read about a human being whose situation is entirely free from risk. More sophisticated readers are always able to maintain the requisite degree of aloofness towards characters in fiction, however human their guise and however dangerous their plight.

Looking then at the heroes and heroines he chooses to read about, we are justified in regarding a child's leisure reading as part of his effort to assimilate the attitudes and values which pertain to the role and status appropriate to his age, sex and social situation. At different stages in his biological growth, he is under pressure to abandon modes of conduct stigmatised as immature, and to assume a more mature role. He is aware of the superior status of those older than himself, and covetous of the increased freedom and power they appear to enjoy. Pressures, therefore, both within and without, thrust him forward through successive phases in his social growth, and, to judge from the changes discernible in children's reading tastes between the ages of six and twelve, this process of social adaptation is marked by three fairly clear stages. Until the age of seven or eight, their chief concern is to explore the requirements of the role imposed on them as young, dependent, powerless members of a family essentially controlled by adults. At this stage, the wider community is regarded either as hostile, and therefore to be shunned, or simply as an extended family in which the code which operates within the home is equally valid. Later, until the age of eleven or twelve, their reading indicates their main concern to be to understand, and to equip themselves to meet, the expectations of their peers. They learn to recognise the norms culturally prescribed as fitting to their age and sex, and become aware of the sometimes conflicting demands of friends and adults. Finally, at the approach of adolescence, their reading shows them attempting to anticipate the adjustments which entry into adult life will require of them.

Between successive phases there is a period of transition attended on the one hand by eagerness to reach out for the wider privileges of the new condition, and on the other by fears of failure and inadequacy. In order to resolve this dilemma, a child may resort to day-dreaming or to reading. Fantasy, it has been said,[1] is at once the necessary preparation for action and the means of delaying it, and at least at these transitional periods in a child's life, reading performs very similar functions. Books offer the young reader a wide variety of identities to be assumed at will, and thus present him with the means of exercise in roles which inner promptings and social pressures both urge him to accept. At the same time, the vicarious satisfactions he achieves in his assumed identity serve to compensate him for the frustration that attends his failure to make the requisite adjustment in reality. Clearly, therefore, while his reading may form a useful part of the child's preparation for a forward step in his social and emotional development, too protracted an interest in heroes or heroines of one kind may be a sign of his evading the task of growing up.

---

[1] Griffiths (1932), p. 292.

CHAPTER V

FANTASY, ROMANCE AND REALISM

WE have seen that for children reading can be the means of self-realisation; through playing a variety of roles, they become more fully aware of their true needs and desires, potentialities and limitations. But apart from helping the child to discover his own identity, it is obvious that reading performs other functions in his life, and above all that of enabling him to explore, and come to terms with, his external environment. This is not to say that children, any more than adults, always read with conscious purpose. Sometimes, of course, and especially when we read works of information—history, geography, travel, science—it is with the express aim of extending our knowledge of the world and of bringing order and significance to what we know ; but when reading fiction, for example, we may not be aware that the underlying purpose of our reading is to bring within our compass as much experience as possible, and to render that experience intelligible to ourselves. Our need to move with confidence and safety in the world around drives us to discern rhythm, pattern and logic in the phenomena we observe in nature and society. What renders the world as it is portrayed in books attractive to us is precisely that it has such rhythm, pattern and logic, imposed by art upon reality. In the same way, part of the appeal which such tales as *The Three Bears* have for the very young lies in their recurrent pattern, and if, as often happens, children resent the slightest change even to the wording of these stories, it is because such changes threaten the predictability, the inevitable order, which is the charm of the story-book world.

It will help us, therefore, to understand the changes that overtake children's reading as they grow, if we regard their reading as part of an attempt to comprehend their physical and social environment. This obviously does not mean that the only books a child will read are those which deal with matters within his personal experience. Beyond the field of which he has immediate knowledge he is aware, from hints, reports and portents, of another world into which sooner or later he will be called upon to fare. His imagination is engaged in formulating

96

an image of that world and in rehearsing the adjustments that he may
have to make. His reading serves as an auxiliary to his imagination :
of both he requires that they should help him to fore-arm for the
encounters he expects to make. Some of the books he reads will deal
with the world with which he is familiar, and his interest in them stems
from his need to comprehend his own experience ; other books he
reads because they afford him insight into unknown worlds, strange
experiences and new problems.

As we have observed, in the process of growing, readers tend to
identify themselves with characters of their own age or somewhat
older. We noticed, too, that the social *milieu* they explore through
their reading tends to widen as they grow : in turn the family, the peer
group, the adult world attract their attention. In much the same way
they may be seen to extend, through their reading, their understanding
of their physical surroundings. Not only through the books they read
on science or on practical subjects, but also through their stories, they
push ever further back their geographical horizons.

Of course, not every book has a precise setting : books on stamp-
collecting or engineering, for example, though obviously concerned
with explaining the external world, may have no exact location ;
moreover, many of the stories read in early childhood are not set in
the real world at all, but in a world of the imagination, in a fairyland
or wonderland having little or no resemblance to the world in which
the reader as a human being is obliged to live. As readers grow older,
however, they tend increasingly to abandon stories with fantastic
backgrounds, and to seek books which are set in one area or another
of the real world. At the age of six, as is shown in Figure 8, roughly a
quarter of the books chosen by these boys and girls are set in fairyland,
but by the age of nine, such stories have almost disappeared from
among those chosen by the boys, and, though the girls continue to read
them somewhat longer, by the age of eleven they too have almost
completely abandoned them in favour of books with settings which
form part of the real world.

There are other obvious trends. At the age of six, the domestic
scene—the nursery, home or farm—and the familiar countryside
form the background to the bulk of the stories read. These fall out of
favour in later years, quite rapidly among the boys after the age of
eight, later and more slowly among the girls. As they decline, stories
set in villages or small towns rise in popularity, to reach their peak

Figure 8
ANALYSIS OF ISSUES ACCORDING TO SETTING
Issues to Boys

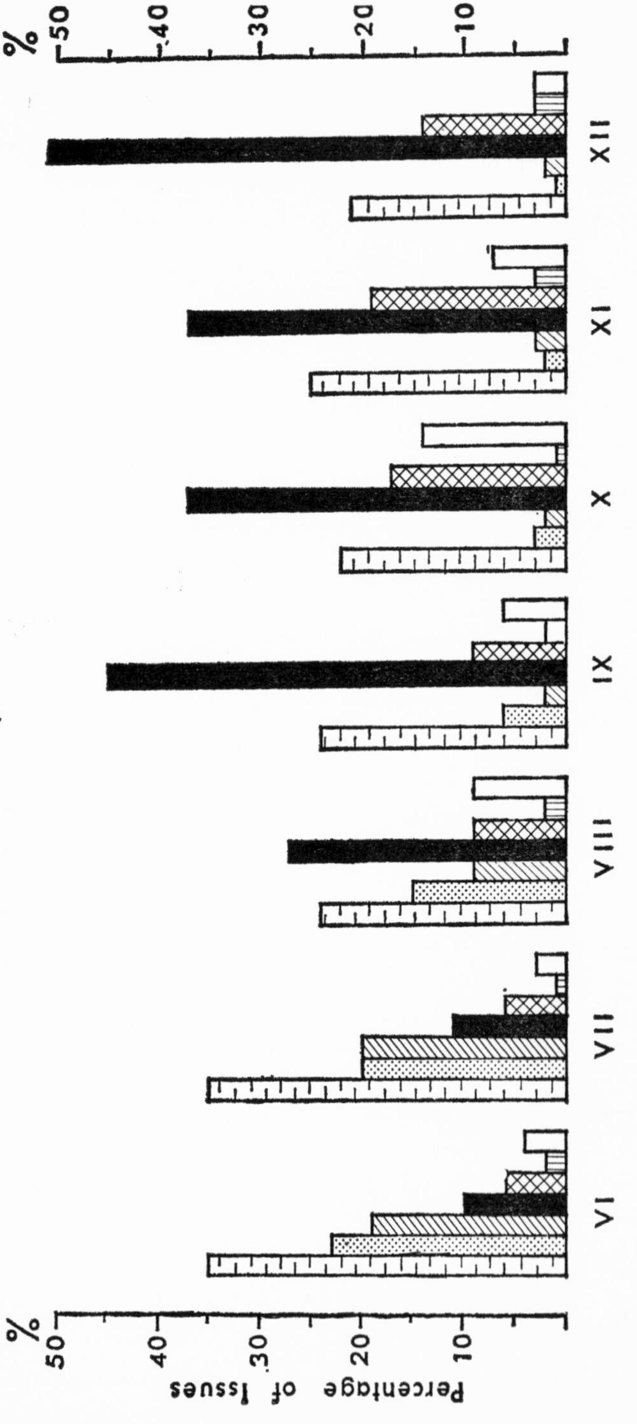

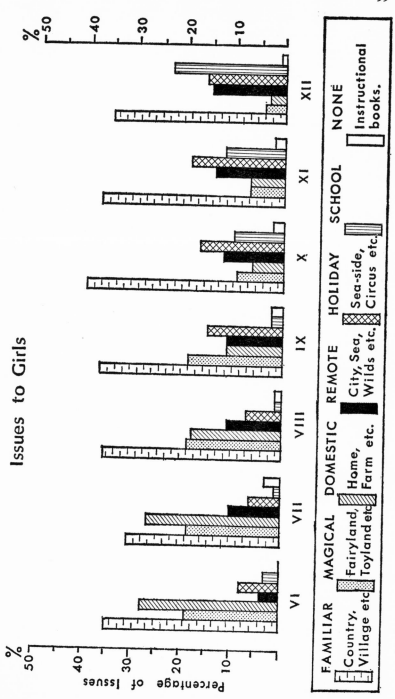

Issues to Girls

with readers ten or eleven years old. With these come stories located in surroundings associated with holidays—at the sea-side, on rivers, in castles and caves, or at the circus. These too appeal most to the ten- and eleven-year-olds, and thereafter start to wane. Among the girls, from about the age of ten, stories with a school setting grow rapidly more popular until they comprise more than a fifth of those borrowed by the girls aged twelve. At no time, however, do they have more than a slight appeal for the boys. Increasingly after the age of eight, their tastes turn towards stories set in the wilds, on sea, in the air, or in outer space. Stories of this kind, which transport their readers to worlds outside the confines of their every-day experience, account for two-fifths of those chosen by the boys aged twelve.

It is clear from Figure 8 that the books which children choose are of two kinds—those which deal with surroundings with which the readers are themselves familiar, and those which present an unfamiliar world, whether it be a world of fantasy or merely some remote or exotic part of the real world. Through their reading, therefore, children either investigate and render comprehensible to themselves their immediate environment, or in imagination probe beyond, leaving behind what is immediate and familiar, and thrusting forward to what is remote and unknown.

It may clarify for us the underlying motives of this imaginative reconnaissance to look again at the rise in popularity of stories with a school background. The great majority of these deal with secondary schools. They are rarely read before the age of ten, but at that age, shortly before they themselves embark upon the secondary stage of their school careers, the girls suddenly begin to read them in considerable numbers. Plainly, therefore, at this stage their readers regard them as offering some sort of preview of the world into which they expect shortly to be plunged. However, these stories retain their popularity among the girls in their first year at the secondary school and even longer. Now, obviously, they serve a somewhat different purpose, that of enabling their readers to comprehend the new environment, to understand its structure and its laws.

What is true of their stories is also true of the works of information they enjoy. Sheena Morey's *Old MacDonald's Farm*, a simple account of life on a farm, with coloured illustrations of farm animals, is typical of the non-fiction which appeals to the very young. The amount of factual information in such books is usually slight ; their main aim is less to instruct than to give expression to their readers' desire to move freely in the world outside the home. Somewhat older readers enjoy *Out with Romany by Meadow and Stream* by G. B. Evens, or *Adventures with the Zoo Man* by David Seth-Smith, while at about the age of nine children come to appreciate such books as *Animal Life in the East* by F. M. and L. J. Duncan.

This survey of the geography, as we may call it, of children's books illustrates certain of the functions which readers, consciously or otherwise, expect their books to serve : that of rendering the familiar comprehensible, and that of introducing, and allaying their anxieties with regard to, the unknown. When we come to look at their themes —the subjects they treat and the incidents they relate—it is again clear that children are concerned on the one hand with matters within their own experience, and on the other with those beyond their actual, but within their fore-seeable, experience. A story of romantic love, however simply told, will fail to hold the reader who is too young to envisage himself in that predicament, whereas an account of children in their dealings with their parents may gain his attention because it has some relevance to his own emotional preoccupations. At the other end of the scale, the girl of twelve is no longer mainly preoccupied with her relations with her parents ; rather is she involved in situations with her age-mates, though already she feels the first stirrings of an interest in the opposite sex. At this stage she may no longer read the simple Family story, but may not be indifferent to a tale of love.

In effect, a child's choice of themes and subjects keeps pace with his emotional development. This follows naturally from what was observed in the last chapter of the tendency on the part of readers to identify themselves with progressively older characters. It emerges, too, from the account given in Chapter II of the kinds of books they are prone to select at various stages, when it was shown how in the estimation of the girls, for instance, the Puppet Story is supplanted by the Fairy Story, and this in turn gives way to School and Mystery Stories, which will themselves ultimately be ousted by the Careers Story and the Adolescent Novel. The trend is clearly towards books which deal with adult rather than childish situations, problems and experiences. The fact that death by violence occurs in only two per cent of the books borrowed by the boys aged six, but in 38 per cent of those read at the age of twelve points in the same direction. Yet another indication is the fact that love or marriage is described in only three per cent of the books chosen by the girls of eight, but in eleven per cent of those read by the girls of twelve.

The image of the world with which children are presented in their books can never be completely faithful to reality. An author may, indeed, intend an accurate portrayal of the external world, but the whole truth is beyond his compass, and the need to select his material itself entails a certain falsity of emphasis, and its arrangement imposes some measure of stylization and convention. Nevertheless, a valid distinction can be made between a work which deserves to be called realistic, in that it contains nothing but the truth, though not the whole truth, and the work of fantasy, in which the author deliberately presents objects or incidents such as do not observably occur in real life. The fact that a story, in certain of its aspects, is at odds with reality does not preclude it from having an underlying fidelity to the truth of human experience. An element of fantasy in the portrayal of character, background and incident may yet be consonant with a genuine attempt to describe authentic motives, values and relationships. The rabbit dressed in human clothes, in a situation which is admittedly incongruous, may nevertheless behave in a completely self-consistent fashion, and serve to illustrate a valid conception of human existence. Another distinction needs to be made : between the realistic and the fantastic stands the romantic picture. In this the separate ingredients are all derived from observable reality, but so selected, and thrown into such high relief as seriously to mis-represent the pattern of normal experience. The common-place and the familiar are ignored, or relegated to a place of no importance ; the novel and extraordinary are elevated to a prominence out of all proportion to their incidence in real life.

Defined in these terms, Fantasy includes Puppet Stories and Fairy Stories, since quite evidently their characters and many of their incidents are such as are never met in nature. Romance takes in Mystery and Adventure stories, since these may be said to distort by false emphasis things which can and do exist in reality. Mystery and danger, for example, certainly form part of human experience, but their incidence in these stories is out of all proportion to their occurrence in every-day life. The category termed Realism may be further sub-divided into Juvenile Realism on the one hand and Adult Realism on the other. The former comprises School Stories, Gang Stories and

Pony Stories, all of which attempt a faithful portrayal of children in their relationships with other children ; the latter includes Family Stories, Careers Stories and Adolescent Novels, all of which try to present an authentic picture of young people in their dealings with the grown-up world.

To look again at Figure 5[1] is to see that the changes which overtake children's reading tastes as they grow older follow a clear and developing pattern. The Fantasy which dominates their reading at the age of six slowly yields to Romance and Realism, to disappear from the boys' repertory after the age of nine, though still present among the girls' choices at the age of twelve. Juvenile Realism, represented by the Gang Story, makes its appearance among the boys' books at the age of six, to gain ground gradually and very slowly throughout the ensuing years. It appears slightly later among the girls' selections, but develops much more rapidly, especially after the age of nine, until by the age of twelve it accounts for one-third of all their reading. Romance, in the form of the Adventure Story, enters the boys' reading programme at the age of seven, and soon threatens to oust all other form of reading, since by the age of eleven the Mystery Story and the Adventure Story together account for four-fifths of all the books borrowed. Once again the girls lag a little behind the boys ; Mystery Stories are first borrowed in appreciable numbers at the age of eight, but they quickly rise in popularity, until at the age of twelve the Mystery Story and the Adventure Story account for a further third of all the books borrowed, thus equalling stories of Juvenile Realism. Adult Realism, as represented by the Family Story, has a place in children's reading from the age of six. With the boys, however, it makes no headway, and after the age of eight is almost entirely neglected. It is otherwise with the girls ; as they grow older they show increasing interest in this kind of story ; more and more Family Stories are read, and to these are added at the age of eleven the Careers Story and the Adolescent Novel, so that more than one-fifth of the books they borrow at the age of twelve fall into this class.

At different stages in their search for a satisfying image of the world, children veer from one mode of presentation to another : from the Fantasy of the Puppet Story to the Realism of the School Story, from the Romance of the Mystery to the Adult Realism of the Careers

[1]Chapter II, p. 38.

story. Fantasy, Juvenile Realism, Romance and Adult Realism, in that order, are the successive steps in their progress towards mature reading tastes.

This tendency for older children to demand a greater degree of realism is evidenced in various ways. They expect their authors to be more realistic, for example, in the portrayal of their characters. An attempt is made, in Figure 9, to show how children's tastes change in this respect from year to year. Certain of the books they read, books of poetry and works of information, contain no living characters ; the remainder are classified according to the nature of the characters they describe. In the first place we have books peopled by creatures of fantasy—puppets, humanised animals, fairies and magical beings. It sometimes happens that one or more of the characters in such a book is an ordinary child, who may well be the central figure, but if the society which the book describes is made up of toys or fairies, then the book is allocated to this class. A second group comprises books which deal with a world of real animals ; Jack London's *Call of the Wild*, Anna Sewell's *Black Beauty*, and Rene Guillot's *Sama* are well-known examples. Next come books containing human characters described in romantic terms. Mystery and Adventure stories obviously form the bulk of those which come within this category, but occasionally in works of non-fiction dealing with historical events, travel or exploration the characters are of heroic stature, or otherwise endowed with qualities and characteristics rarely found in the people their readers encounter in their daily lives. This is the criterion which distinguishes these from the realistic human characters who commonly, though not invariably, appear in School Stories, Family Stories and Careers Stories.

It will be seen from Figure 9 that books in which the characters are essentially figures of fantasy are enormously popular among the six-year-olds, but fall rapidly out of favour, especially after the age of nine or ten. As they decline, books in which the characters are portrayed in romantic guises are borrowed in increasing numbers. At the same time, there is a tendency, particularly among the girls, for readers to borrow as they grow older more and more books dealing with realistic characters. Books describing the world of real animals never enjoy more than a moderate popularity, and their numbers dwindle as the children grow older. The books which children borrow at the age of six are unequally divided between those whose characters are

creatures of fantasy and those containing realistic human beings ; at
the age of twelve, their books are again of two kinds : those with
romantic, and those with realistic, human characters. In the intervening
years romance gradually replaces fantasy in the books these children
borrow.

It was said earlier that the order of progression in children's reading
is from Fantasy to Juvenile Realism, thence to Romance, and finally to
Adult Realism. This, however, over-simplifies the process. The
transition from one phase to another is never abrupt or clear-cut,
either in the development of children as a whole or in the history of
any individual. To illustrate this, one need only point to the range
and variety among the books borrowed by the girls of twelve. It
would not be difficult, either, to point to individual readers who
borrow from the Library a Careers Story one week and a Mystery
Story the next. When choosing a book, the reader may have one of a
number of purposes in mind, and it is his purpose for reading which
determines his choice of subject, and, more specifically, the sort of
treatment he expects the subject to be given. He may choose a book
about Red Indians, for example, for purposes of information or
entertainment. If the former is his aim, however, he is likely to look
for a much more realistic treatment of Red Indians than when reading
for pure pleasure. In other words, whether a child chooses a work of
Fantasy, Romance, or Realism depends upon the purposes for which
he reads.

To illustrate the role played by Fantasy in children's reading, it
may be as well to take a close look at a story typical of many of those
borrowed by the six-year-olds. In Beatrix Potter's *Tale of Samuel
Whiskers*, little Tommy Kitten mischievously hides from his mother,
only to be captured by Samuel Whiskers the rat, who with his wife
decides to make him into kitten dumpling. They steal the necessary
butter, dough and rolling-pin, and have already encased him in dough
when Tommy's mother brings the farmer to the rescue. Tommy is
restored to the safety of his home, while the two rats are forced to
decamp in haste to another farm. Clearly implied, though not overtly
stated, as it might have been in stories of an earlier day, is the moral
that the home and the community are places of security and happiness
for those who obey the appropriate rules of conduct. It may be
questioned, however, whether the young reader is so much concerned
to learn such salutary lessons as to overcome in imagination the

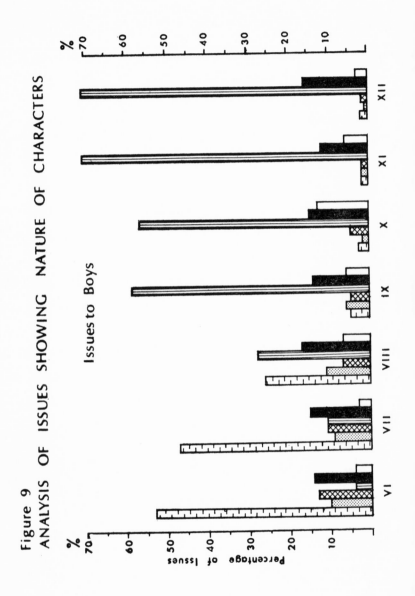

Figure 9
ANALYSIS OF ISSUES SHOWING NATURE OF CHARACTERS

Issues to Boys

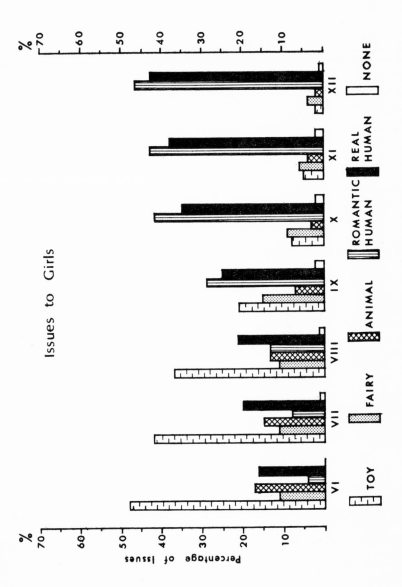

apprehensions which prevent him from making similar experiments in real life. Here, the deliberate absence of realism serves to guard the reader against too close and unpleasant an involvement with the characters and their predicament. Fantasy, that is to say, here serves the purpose of allaying the reader's fears and anxieties.

The need for such protective mechanisms is strongest when the story involves the characters in hazards, physical or emotional. The threat of danger is fairly common in these stories, but is rarely realized. Violent death occurs, as we have said, in only two per cent of the stories borrowed at the age of six, and even when, as is more frequently the case, the threat is to the happiness and emotional security of the characters, the outcome of the story is invariably happy. In many, the part of *deus ex machina* is played by parents or other adults, but in others, as in the fairy-tales which are often among the most harrowing of the stories read by children at this early age, a happy issue is brought about by magic. One facet of children's addiction to fantasy at this time is their fondness for stories with some element of magic. Miraculous events occur in nearly a quarter of the books borrowed at the age of six. Afterwards, the boys borrow fewer and fewer of these stories every year, until by the age of twelve they are seldom borrowed by the boys ; the girls, however, read them in increasing numbers until the age of nine, but by the age of twelve the girls read them almost as rarely as the boys.

Beatrix Potter's *Tale of Samuel Whiskers* is fairly representative of the works of fantasy enjoyed by boys and girls aged six. In the great majority of the books they read at this age there is a deliberate absence of realism in the setting of the story, in the beings who inhabit it, or in the happenings which are described. A substantial minority of the books read at this age, however, are of a different kind. These belong for the most part to the category of the Family Story, and describe in reasonably credible and realistic terms the activities of an ordinary child in or near the home. Sheena Morey's *Old MacDonald's Farm*, outlined earlier in this chapter, is typical of these. It differs from Beatrix Potter's story not only in being more realistic but also because its atmosphere is untroubled and serene. Even more important is the fact that it deals with matters within the range of its readers' own experience.

Until the age of eight or nine, then, children's choices among books are divided between those which deal in fairly realistic terms with subjects closely related to their own experience, and those which deal in the idiom of fantasy with situations of a kind they have not yet encountered in their daily life. Before entering school, a child's first-hand experience is extremely narrow ; nearly all the things he reads about will be unfamiliar to him, and, in consequence, the only realistic books he reads will tend to be those which deal with the home life of a young child. Frances Ingersoll's *Peter Gets His Wish* is an example of this kind of story, and is often read by five-year-olds. At this age, however, children tend to read about remote school-life in Puppet Stories such as Jane Pilgrim's *Ernest Owl Starts a School*, or Rodney Bennett's *Little Miss Pink's School*, or Irma Wilde's *The Giraffe who went to School*. At the age of six or seven, they are prepared for more realistic accounts of school experience, such as Enid Blyton's *Benjy and the Others*, or Kathryn and Byron Jackson's *Jerry at School*, but are still prone to choose Aesopian stories such as Lillian Miozzi's *The Adventures of Tommy, the cat who went to sea* when they wish to read about the world beyond.

A dialectical progression, therefore, seems to underlie this vacillation between fantasy and realism. Before the age of eight or nine, the reader makes his first approach to fields of unfamiliar experience by the avenue of fantasy ; he gradually acquires confidence for a more direct approach by way of realism to the zone thus reconnoitred, and in the meantime probes still further afield by means of fantasy. It is true, of course, that except within a limited sphere of his own experience, the young reader has no criteria by which to judge of the veracity or otherwise of the accounts given to him in books, but it is also true that he is prepared to accept, or even to prefer, a high degree of obvious artifice in the treatment of unfamiliar subjects. It may be supposed that in the first place this adds to his immunity, and in the second it affords him more freedom to mould the fictional experience to his own requirements. The reader is no passive recipient of the image impressed on him by books : he is unconsciously engaged in selecting and re-shaping it to his own needs. And the symbolic figure, the caricature or cartoon, is often preferred because it lends itself more easily to imaginative re-interpretation than does the rigidly realistic figure. For much the same reasons, young children often prefer to play with an undistinguished piece of wood rather than with the elaborate and expensive toy.

For the boys, their eighth year is clearly a period of transition between the reading interests of childhood and those of boyhood. Even before this age, their reading has come to reflect a certain impatience with the limitations imposed upon their freedom, a certain longing for power and independence, a temptation to flout the rules of social and domestic life, and a desire to cock a snook at common-sense itself. Before the age of eight, however, it is through the medium of fantasy that the boys give vent to this spirit of rebellion. The stories of Muffin the Mule by Ann Hogarth and Annette Mills, which are less difficult to read but otherwise not unlike the Pooh tales of A. A. Milne, are fairly typical of those they choose at this stage. The central figure is a toy mule living with other toy animals in a world broadly modelled on the human world. Muffin is their leader and the acknowledged arbiter of life in this community. He has no family ties and is subject to no constraint. He possesses magical powers, and his actions, however eccentric or absurd, are accepted without question by the others. The humour that pervades these stories is derived from the parodying of adult orderliness, solemnity and rationality. From the age of eight onwards, however, the boys express their impatience of childish restrictions more and more through their reading of romance. Incidents connected with war, hazardous exploration, crime, capture and escape, death by violence, all appear much more frequently than hitherto in the books which they select, and there is a notable increase in the element of mystery. There is a corresponding decline in the place given in their stories to common-place events, to childish pursuits, and to domestic and social activities. The change is reflected also in the tendency for boys of this age to choose stories set in exotic places—on the high seas, in the wilds, or in foreign cities—rather than in the prosaic surroundings of home, village or countryside. Interest in fantasy survives. Magical and irrational incidents occur as frequently as in the books chosen by the boys of seven. In turning to romance, it is not the fantastic that these readers are rejecting, but the common-place.

Another aspect of the change that comes about at this time is the sharp growth of interest in works of information, and especially in books of nature-study and wild life. At the age of eight, the boys borrow proportionately twice as many works of non-fiction as in the previous year, the majority of them scientific books, but almost equally as many dealing with hobbies and leisure-time activities, chiefly of an outdoor nature. Interest is also high in subjects pertaining to engineering and mechanics, in locomotives, motor-cars, ships and air-craft, and for the first time biographies appear among the books selected by the boys.

By the age of nine the emergence from childhood into boyhood is virtually complete. Henceforward Fantasy has no place in the boys' reading ; animated toys and animals have almost completely disappeared from their books, and stories of beings with magical or supernatural attributes are quite out of favour. Certain of the themes which hitherto have been prominent are no longer of great concern ; not only are the books they choose less preoccupied with magical, fantastic and humorous incidents, but fewer of them are concerned with family and social relationships. What is perhaps most characteristic of the nine-year-old boys is their fondness for tales of capture and escape, and these, together with other tales of violent adventure involving adult characters, grow increasingly popular in the following years, to eclipse even the Mystery Story by the age of twelve. Through his reading of such stories a boy gives vent to thwarted urges for independence, domination and aggression, but it is perhaps even more indicative of his desire for initiation to the world of men and for participation in men's experience. At the same time there is a great deal of covert curiosity about grown-up behaviour and its motives, and this finds an outlet chiefly in the reading of Mystery Stories. The remaining choices of boys at this stage fall upon Gang Stories on the one hand and works of information on the other. These seem to be part of a more realistic and practical attempt to widen the scope of their activities and experience, and to make effective adjustments to the outside world and to the other children who are now their principal companions.

Changes similar to those which occur among the boys at the age of eight take effect later and more gradually among the girls. From the age of nine their taste for Fantasy declines, and at the same time they borrow fewer books in which the action is confined to the limits of the home. They do not share the boys' taste for stories set at sea or in the wilds, but like them seem to expect of their stories an introduction to a wider world, free from adult domination. School stories begin to be popular with the girls aged ten. Teachers play only a minor part in these stories, which deal for the most part with the activities of groups of girls ruled entirely by their prefects or their own appointed leaders and obedient to codes of conduct of their own devising. Not unexpectedly, tales of mischief, of youthful pranks in defiance of adult authority, enjoy considerable favour at this stage. From the age of nine onwards their reading interests suggest that the girls have a growing desire to free themselves from dependence upon adults, and look increasingly to their peers for satisfying personal relations, for approval and acceptance. This is reflected in their new liking for tales of sport, and especially of horse-riding. The Pony Stories widely read at this stage lay great stress upon the qualities which makes a child acceptable, or give it status, in the group. At the same time, the underlying theme in many is the strong emotional relationship between its human owner and the horse. For the readers of these books, mastery over a horse serves as a symbol of emergence from dependent childhood into an age of freedom, responsibility and power. Moreover, their first yearning for some more uniquely personal relationship than is possible between members of a family finds expression in their liking for stories of deep love between a young person and an animal, usually a horse. Human love between the sexes does not appear prominently in the books selected by the ten-year-olds. The reading of Pony Stories is an indirect and guarded approach to that theme. The girls of this age are clearly aware of themselves as on the threshold of adult life, and their curiosity about that way of life reflects itself obliquely in their intense interest in books containing an element of mystery. Nearly one-third of the books chosen by the girls aged ten relate the exploits of groups of youngsters investigating mysterious circumstances or trying to penetrate the secretive behaviour of grown-ups.

These are some of the new themes which increasingly occupy the girls from the age of nine. Other more obviously adult themes also make their appearance at this stage and play an increasingly prominent part in the girls' reading as they grow older. Although stories entirely devoted to romantic love are rarely among those they borrow, courtship, love and marriage play an incidental part in many of the Adolescent Novels and Careers Stories chosen by the older girls, the central themes of which turn upon an adolescent's experience of family life, of work, and of community relationships. It is here that the main differences lie between the reading interests of the boys and of the girls. Broadly speaking, the boys as they grow older are concerned to explore through their reading the material world, the world of sensory experience and of physical action. The girls, in contrast, are more concerned with the world of human beings, their mutual adjustments and relationships.

In one important respect, however, the development of the boys runs the same course as that of the girls. When at the age of eight or nine childhood is left behind, Fantasy is abandoned for Romance. Once again the books chosen by these boys and girls fall into two broad classes : the realistic, dealing for the most part with people, places, activities and relationships of the kind with which readers of this age are occupied in real life ; and the romantic, which express for them a vision of life beyond the limits of their own experience. Themes related to activities away from home, to school life, to youthful mischief, to the exploits of the gang, which readers have hitherto broached chiefly through the medium of fantasy, are now presented in straight-forward terms, while adult activities and relationships—work, the maintenance of law and order, leadership and loyalty—are tolerated only when invested with the glamour of romance in stories of adventure, outlawry and detection. The older girls advance beyond this stage when they begin to accept a more realistic treatment of these themes in their Careers Stories and Adolescent Novels, but before the age of thirteen few of the boys appear to be prepared to take this step.

Fantasy and Romance both appear therefore to be means whereby readers at different stages of development advance the frontiers of experience. They differ in that they give expression to two contrasted attitudes on the part of children towards the unknown. An individual's emotional response to the new and strange is always compounded of curiosity and fear, and in the youngest, for whom security tends to be the prime concern, timidity predominates and dictates that all approaches to the unfamiliar should be made tentatively and with safeguards. Their preference for Fantasy is symptomatic of their reluctance to venture beyond the reassuringly familiar. To older children the outside world, even that of which they have no immediate knowledge, is not so awesome and mysterious ; on the contrary, they have come to regard the barriers between themselves and the unknown less as a means to their protection than as an irksome hindrance to their freedom. Their enthusiasm for Romance, the zest with which in fiction they encounter adventure, mystery and danger, bear witness to their boredom and frustration with the safe and the familiar.

If Fantasy and Romance are the forms in which readers at

different stages prefer to encounter new experience, Realism is looked to to provide satisfying interpretations of what is already known. Works of non-fiction serve this purpose by classifying and explaining phenomena in the physical and material world ; works of fiction do so by uncovering motives, relationships, causes and effects in the field of human behaviour. The taste for realism in fiction springs neither from anxiety nor frustration ; rather it arises from a much more practical desire on the part of the reader to comprehend the logic of his own experience and to make more effective adjustments to it.

What we have tried to emphasise is that a child's reading should not be regarded in isolation, but as part of his total effort to cope with his circumstances. At each stage of his growth, the child is involved in new relationships, meets new emotional problems, fresh difficulties of adjustment. At the age of six, for instance, he is concerned with finding freedom with security in the narrow circle of his home ; at nine he is torn between obedience to his elders and allegiance to his peers ; at twelve he is anxious to learn how to make himself acceptable to those grown-up men among whom soon he will have to work and find companionship. These and similar preoccupations appropriate to each age will be reflected in the books he reads. Thus among the books he chooses at the age of six will be *Boo, the boy who didn't like the dark, Pookie in search of a home,* and *The little engine that ran away*. At nine, he joins Richmal Crompton's William in cocking a snook at the grown-ups who hedge him round. At twelve he identifies himself with the youthful heroes who prove their manhood in the stories of Eric Leyland and Percy F. Westerman.

For the healthy reader reading is a form of exploration. Beset by a problem in life, he sends forward his imagination into fiction to chart a way forward through the difficulties. His progress in life is one of ready adjustment to successive situations and to an ever-widening range of human relationships, and this is reflected in his reading by a similar steady progress from books dealing with childish problems of adjustment to the home, father, mother and brothers, to those which deal with man's concern with the great problems of life, death, love, pain and immortality. The problem when he first approaches it in books may be disguised in fantasy or romance. Gradually he comes to accept a greater degree of realism. Ideally this would lead to a more complete appraisal of the problem and to its ultimate solution in his daily life. The unhealthy reader, on the other hand, reads not on the advance but in retreat. Defeated by a problem in life he seeks in books, not a solution to his difficulties, but a refuge from them. In his reading he never progresses beyond a given theme, he rests chiefly in the zone of romance, rarely sallies into realism, readily turns to fantasy and to books intended for younger readers.

The second point to be stressed follows naturally from this. Good reading is primarily, perhaps, but not entirely, a matter of ' good ' books. A child should derive both pleasure and profit from his reading. The pleasure he gains from reading a book comes from the fact that it allows him to live vicariously a life at once richer and less confusing than his own. The profit will depend on whether it equips him to face his own life with increased confidence, self-control and under-standing. This itself depends in part upon his reading in a critical, inquiring spirit, rather than in a passive or escapist fashion. In part, also, it depends upon some quality of truth within the books them-selves, however incomplete, simplified or allegorical it be. In addition to all this, the books he reads must be the right books, books which illuminate his own predicament, and are appropriate to his stage of emotional development. Good reading, in short, is reading which helps the reader to mature.

CHAPTER VI

MEMBERS AND NON-MEMBERS

IN the foregoing chapters we have studied voluntary reading as a continuous process in the lives of children. Knowing that the newly-born do not read at all, and knowing that among adults the reading of books is widespread, we have tried to trace the steps by which, in the intervening years, the habit takes hold and spreads. Our findings are recorded in Chapter I. We know also that the reading tastes of young children differ in important ways from those of older people. In other chapters we have tried to record the separate stages of the transformation that takes place between infancy and adolescence. We have observed these children as they grow become increasingly prepared to accept books which make ever greater demands upon their reading powers. We have traced their gradual abandonment of the themes of infancy and childhood, and their growing interest in situations and problems proper to adolescence and maturity. We have traced their progress from fantasy, through romance, towards that realism which adults generally demand.

Inevitably in all this we have directed our attention to central tendencies, to the averages, means and norms characteristic of children of a given age, and have tended to neglect the wide differences that separate one child from another of the same age, differences often greater than those between one age-group and another. We claim to have discerned certain patterns and sequences amid the welter of choices that children make among books. The fact remains, however, that one child of ten borrows 165 books in a year while others of that age borrow none at all. Again, one girl of twelve is content to read stories of excursions into fairyland, while another chooses books in which the themes and the degree of realism with which the themes are treated would not be out of place in an adult novel.

Such variations are a matter of common observation, and if we have so far neglected them, it is because they are better understood when seen against the general trends from which they are deviations. In order to understand them we must ask ourselves why one reader should read so many more or fewer books than is usual among children of his age, why another should choose books markedly more or less difficult, much more or less mature in their themes, much more realistic or fantastic in their treatment. In the chapters which follow we shall try to find answers to these questions, and in order to do so, we shall focus our attention upon a much smaller group than hitherto, namely, upon the 369 children who at the time of the enquiry were in the last year of their primary, or the first year of their secondary, education. Their ages on May 1st of the school year in which their reading was recorded ranged from 10 years 6 months to 12 years 11 months.

We shall begin by trying to discover what distinguishes the 60 per cent who join the Library from the 40 per cent who do not.

Sex Differences

One obvious factor is sex. As Table 1 shows, although the group as a whole is almost equally divided between the sexes, among members of the Library the girls outnumber the boys in a ratio of three to two. The great majority of those who fail to join the Library are boys.

	Boys		Girls		Both	
	No.	%	No.	%	No.	%
Members	89	24	132	36	221	60
Non-Members	96	26	52	14	148	40
	185	50	184	50	369	100
Chi Square 21.9 , P <.001						

TABLE 1. Membership of the Library according to Sex.

This is roughly consonant with what we have seen to happen in every age-group other than at nine, and accords, moreover, with what almost every observer of children's reading has noted, that girls are more given to reading than are boys.

The simplest explanation is that boys have many more other things to do than have the girls. Certainly in the provision of clubs and of facilities for outdoor activities, boys in this country[1] are much more fortunate than their sisters. Again, as was suggested earlier, in some sections of society, and notably among manual workers, whose children after all form the majority, reading is regarded as an activity more appropriate to girls than boys. It is also possible that the books available are lacking in appeal for boys. If there is a shortage of books suitable for boys, it is not confined to this library, but must be widespread if it is to account for the fact that boys have almost everywhere been found to read less than girls. Whatever the initial causes of this state of affairs, it is all too likely that authors and publishers, in pursuit of the biggest markets, will tend to perpetuate it by providing books for girls rather than for boys. There is some evidence[2] to support the common-sense view that it is the child who is able to read well who on the whole will read for pleasure, and it has often been claimed that girls perform better at tests of reading ability than do boys. On neither score, however, is the testimony unequivocal,[3] and on balance, therefore, the most plausible explanations of sex differences in reading habits are those which take into account the unequal recreational opportunities, the possible dearth of books suitable for boys, and the cultural pressures which cause reading to be regarded as effeminate.

Library Membership and Educational Attainment

The children who join the Library differ from the rest in another respect: they tend to be more successful in school work. As Table 2 shows, a considerably higher proportion of members than of non-members were either already admitted to the grammar school or qualified for admission in the following year. Roughly one in two of the members, but only one in three of the non-Members is of grammar school standard.

This is not unexpected. All the available evidence goes to show

---

[1]In the U.S.A., also, there seems to be a wider range of diversions for boys, with the result that more girls than boys mention reading as a favourite pastime. See Coleman (1961), p. 369.

[2]Ladd (1933, p. 26) reports a correlation of $+.30$ between number of books read and reading achievement, and concludes that reading ability is of greater importance than intelligence in determining the amount of voluntary reading.

[3]Brearley (1949, p. 180) finds that reading habits depend little on reading skill. Ladd, Vernon and McLaren unlike Burt, Ballard and Fleming, find no consistent differences between boys and girls in reading ability.

that the more successful children read more than others.[1] This does not necessarily mean that voluntary reading, or more specifically membership of the library, makes for better performance at school, though this may well be true. The effects are probably reciprocal, success at school fostering an interest in reading, and the habit of voluntary reading having a beneficial effect upon school work. Conversely, failure to read outside school may affect adversely school performance, and lack of success at school tends to destroy all interest in books.

	Grammar Standard		Secondary Modern Standard		All	
	No.	%	No.	%	No.	%
Members	94	72	93	51	187	60
Non-Members	37	28	89	49	126	40
	131	100	182	100	313	100
	Chi Square 13.96 ; P <.001					

TABLE 2.   Members and Non-Members according to Educational Standard.

On the evidence given in Table 2, it is reasonable to suppose that there is a clear association between library membership and educational attainment. At the same time, the strength of this association is not the same for boys and girls, as is clear from Table 3, which compares library membership among boys and girls in relation to their educational level.

With boys, that is to say, library membership is significantly higher among those of grammar standard than among those of secondary modern calibre, but with girls the difference is not important. Since this implies that a boy who is unsuccessful at school tends to have no interest in library books, whereas a girl is likely to be as attracted whether she does well at school or not, it may reflect a profound difference between the sexes in their attitude to leisure reading. It suggests that boys tend to associate the library with school, and to

---

[1]In Britain, Jenkinson (1940) offers the most conclusive evidence on this score. For the U.S.A., see Lazar (1937) ; for New Zealand, Scott (1947).

	Boys				Girls			
	Grammar standard		Sec. Mod. standard		Grammar standard		Sec. Mod. standard	
	No.	%	No.	%	No.	%	No.	%
Members	41	64	32	35	53	79	62	67
Non-Members	23	36	57	65	14	21	31	33
	64	100	89	100	67	100	93	100
	Difference 29% Chi Square 11.9 ; P < .001				Difference 12% Chi Square 3.18 ; Not Significant.			

TABLE 3.　Membership of the Library according to Educational Standard. Boys and Girls compared.

regard all forms of reading as to some extent related to school work, while for the girls, on the other hand, the reading of library books seems to be an essentially recreational activity quite unconnected with what they do at school. In more general terms, it implies that the search for pleasure ranks higher as a motive for reading among the girls than among the boys, a conclusion to which others who have considered this question have been drawn.[1]

Library Membership and Intelligence

School performance is known to correlate highly with intelligence scores, and it is not surprising therefore that Library members, who tend to be recruited from those who do comparatively well at school, should have higher intelligence scores on average than those who fail to join. However, just as it is quite common to find grammar school children who do not use the library and secondary modern children who do, so it is by no means unusual to find highly intelligent children who apparently do little or no leisure reading, and others of very low intelligence with a great appetite for books. Indeed, intelligence has not always been found to have any bearing on the matter, and it is

---

[1]Notably Philpott (1953), p. 122.

generally agreed that it is a less important factor than educational attainment.[1] As far as Library members are concerned, at all events, while it is true that they are somewhat more intelligent than others, it is not so much this which marks them off from non-members as the fact that they tend to achieve higher standards of school work. Table 4 classifies library members and others into those with scores, on a non-verbal test of intelligence,[2] of 101 or more, or 100 and below.

	IQ 101 and above		IQ 100 and below	
	No.	%	No.	%
Members	96	65	85	49
Non-Members	52	35	89	51
	—	—	—	—
	148	100	174	100
	Chi Square 8.5 ; P <.01			

TABLE 4. Library Membership according to level of Intelligence.

It will be seen that nearly two-thirds of those who do not join the Library are below average intelligence. Among the members, on the other hand, those of more than average intelligence slightly outnumber the less intelligent. To put it differently, the average intelligence of library members is 100.5, nearly three points higher than that of the entire group, and 5.5 points higher than the average for those who do not join.

The difference is significant (P <.001) and points clearly to the fact that the more intelligent the child, the more likely he or she is to be attracted to the Library. This emerges unmistakeably from Table 5, which shows that the percentage of children joining the Library steadily declines as the level of intelligence declines.

---

[1]The highest correlation between intelligence and voluntary reading (+.4) is that reported by Wollner (1949, p. 78). Positive correlations are also reported by Lipscomb (1931) and Ladd (1933). In an investigation confined to ' C ' stream grammar boys, however, Mullett (1951, p. 56) finds no correlation.

[2]Daniel's Figure Reasoning Test. Mean for entire group 97.88, Standard Deviation 14.97.

The F value for the boys is much higher than for the girls, indicating that among the former library membership is much more dependent upon intelligence than among the latter. The Library succeeds in attracting a relatively high proportion of girls of very low intelligence. One of the two girls with scores of less than 70 is a member, together

IQ	121+	111+	101+	91+	81+	71+	61+
Boys%	67	56	48	42	32	33	0
Girls %	80	79	73	63	64	69	50

Analysis of Variance			Boys	Girls	df.
Variance due to Intelligence			2,470	506	1
Variance due to other factors			290	139	5
		F	49.4	18.3	

TABLE 5. Percentage of children joining the Library at each level of Intelligence.

with nine of the thirteen with scores between 71 and 80. In contrast, none of the five boys with scores of 70 or below is a member, and only four of the twelve in the group immediately above. A surprisingly high proportion of girls of very limited intelligence show what one can only feel is a pathetic eagerness to share, despite the difficulties they no doubt encounter, in an activity which provides a bond with other children.

Library Membership and Social Class

A growing body of evidence suggests[1] that educational attainment and measured intelligence are both strongly influenced by socio-economic factors, and, since library members do relatively well in tests of intelligence and school work, it is tempting to assume that they are drawn predominantly from better-off homes. The idea is obviously not entirely baseless. Carsley (1957), for instance, finds that the proportion of children who join the library is much higher among those who live in residential areas than on housing estates or in areas

---

[1]See, for example, Douglas (1964).

designated as ' Artisan.'[1] Watts (1944) also claims[2] to have found that whereas in a fairly good working-class district more than sixty per cent of the children borrowed regularly from the public library, in a poorer district of the same borough fewer than twenty per cent did so. Brearley (1949), on the other hand, contrasting ' good ' residential areas with ' bad,'[3] finds no significant difference in library attendance among children, while Dunlop (1950) goes even further, claiming[4] that in Glasgow it is the better-off children who make least use of the library facilities available.

By and large, the poorer the district, the less adequate are the library facilities, and this in itself is perhaps sufficient to explain the evidence of Carsley and of Watts. It may well be, however, that given equal opportunities children from poorer homes are as ready as others to make use of libraries. In Llanfair, at all events, the proportion of children visiting the Library is exactly the same for manual as for non-manual workers' children, and this is true for the boys and for the girls. If this should cause surprise, it must be remembered that all the children here considered live within a radius of one mile from the only public library in the town, and that those from poorer homes enjoy therefore exactly the same facilities and opportunities as other children.

This is not to deny that, when other sources of books are taken into account, middle-class children read more than children of the working class. Since on the whole they are more intelligent and more successful at school, it is reasonable to suppose they do, but that they depend less for their books upon the public library than do manual workers' children, who are likely to have fewer books at home. There is no gain-saying that in this as in other respects the good home confers lasting advantages upon its children, and ideally a junior library would aim to make available to all children the books which the most enlightened of parents in the best of homes would provide for their own. Just how close this or any other library comes to this ideal must be a matter of opinion, but its success in reaching children from every type of background is heartening proof that the effort to offset the disadvantages suffered by children from poorer homes is far from vain. Among the measures by which we may hope to remove educational

---

[1]Residential 62% ; Artisan ' A ' 49.7% ; Artisan ' B ' 52%. Housing Estate 26.6%.

[2]p. 106.   [3]p. 170.   [4]p. 96.

and social inequalities, that of ensuring through our schools and public libraries an ample supply of books for every child is by no means the least promising.

Library Membership and Secondary Selection

Naturally enough, children, together with their parents and teachers, will be more concerned with the immediate benefits that reading brings, and tend to expect that diligent attendance at the library will lead to an improvement in school performance. It is not easy to say, however, whether a child joins the library because he does well at school, or whether he does well at school because he joins the library. The probability is, as we have said, that both are true, but it is worth considering further whether being a member benefits a child in academic work, and, more specifically, whether it markedly improves his chances of gaining a grammar school place. Is it the case that, of two children equal in intelligence, the one who makes use of the library is more likely to gain admission than the other?

It is clear that the benefit, if any, will be greatest for those on or near the borderline. The highly intelligent child, whether he uses the library or not, is almost certain to win a place, while at the other extreme the dullest is almost certain to fail. The fate of the remainder, those with intelligence scores between 101 and 120, is more doubtful, with about one in three being successful. In this marginal group, as is shown in Table 6, those who were members of the Library fared rather better than those who were not.

	Successful	Unsuccessful	All
Members	14	17	31
Non-Members	4	17	21
	Chi Square 3.77 ; P <.05		

TABLE 6.   Results of grammar school selection among boys and girls with IQ scores 101 to 120.

Library members among these border-line candidates gained proportionately twice as many places as non-members, and this was true of boys and girls alike. Unfortunately, the numbers involved are too small to put the matter completely beyond doubt, but such as they are, they lend support to the suggestion that joining the library materially improves the chances of a child at the border-line of gaining a grammar school place.

Library Membership and Family Size

To return, however, to the relationship between home background and reading habits, it will be realised that the social status of parents is not the only aspect of home life to have a possible bearing upon a child's attitude to books. The size of the family cannot be ignored. It has often been shown that children from small families make higher scores on tests of intelligence than children from large families, and that they are more successful in gaining grammar school places. If only for these reasons, a higher proportion of them might be expected to join the library. Moreover, whether a child has much time for reading will depend upon the other things which occupy his time, and this depends in part upon the number of other children in the home. When the family is large the girls, if not the boys, are commonly expected to devote some of their time to looking after younger children. Furthermore, as an indoor pastime, reading competes with other activities in which a child can join with his brothers and sisters. On the surface, then, it is the solitary child, or the one with few brothers and sisters who would seem more likely to be interested in reading. Nevertheless, as Table 7 reveals, it is only among the boys that substantial differences appear ; girls from large families join the Library almost as frequently as those from small.

An only child is not appreciably more likely to join the Library than a child with one or two siblings ; it is only when the family has four or more children that it exerts any deterrent effect. This may be connected with the fact that scores on intelligence and attainment tests have been shown to fall considerably when families reach this size.[1] The child who is one of many in the family often suffers certain disadvantages which operate to retard educational progress and also to discourage interest in leisure reading. Lack of privacy and loss of parental interest are among the causes in both cases, and in addition, as was mentioned earlier, it is likely that the child who has many brothers and sisters has other interests and activities competing for his time.

---

[1]Douglas (1964), p. 93.

	Boys		Girls		Boys and Girls	
	No. in Group	Percentage Library Members	No. in Group	Percentage Library Members	No. in Group	Percentage Library Members
Small Families	123	51	137	72	260	62
Large Families	49	29	31	65	80	43
	172	100	168	100	340	100
Difference	22		7		19	
	Chi Square 7.38		Chi Square .77		Chi Square 9.63	
	P <.001		Not significant		P < .001	

TABLE 7.   Library membership among children of large and small families.

Note : Large families are those with four or more children,
       Small families less than four.

Conclusion

We have tried to discover whether the children who join the Library differ from those who do not in level of intelligence and educational attainment, in social class and in family size. In the event, none of these factors proves to be as important as that of sex ; the bulk of children who join are girls, and the majority of those who abstain are boys. Otherwise, library members are chiefly characterised by their relatively high level of attainment in school work and by the high proportion gaining grammar school places. They tend also to be of higher intelligence and to come from families of not more than three children. However, insofar as the girls are concerned, these factors are of only marginal importance ; the great majority of them join the Library, undeterred by low intelligence, poor performance at school, or membership of large families, factors which appear to have adverse effects upon the boys. All this applies to children aged eleven and twelve, and there is no direct evidence to suggest that it is true of others. On the contrary, in earlier years the Library casts its net more widely and draws in many whom it will not retain. Especially at the age of ten, many children enrol for what seems to be a trial period. The ones who later fall away will for the most part be those discouraged by their lack of progress at school and to some extent, perhaps, by the disadvantages associated with large families. Conspicuous among those whose interest it fails to hold are those boys who enter the secondary modern school.

CHAPTER VII

READING INTERESTS AND EDUCATIONAL ATTAINMENT

WE have considered some of the factors which might be thought to have a bearing on a child's decision to join the Library or not, and have found that, apart from the child's age and sex, the one carrying most weight is the standard of the work the child achieves in school ; children who make relatively good progress are more prone to become members than those who do less well. However, the effects of school performance on leisure reading go much further than this. Once having joined the Library, the more able scholars borrow, not only more books, but other kinds of books than the less able.

Education and Volume of Reading

When we consider those members who are in their last year of primary education or their first year of secondary, we find that those whose standard of attainment fits them for the grammar school borrow roughly speaking one more book each month than those who qualify for the secondary modern school. Table 1 gives the average

| | Group 'A' | | Group 'B' | | |
	No. of Readers	Average Books	No. of Readers	Average Books	Difference
Boys					
Primary	15	29.0	23	15.9	13.1
Secondary	21	17.9	7	8.1	9.8
All	36	23.9	30	14.0	9.9*
Girls					
Primary	19	41.8	39	25.3	16.5
Secondary	34	37.7	23	26.7	11.0
All	53	39.2	62	25.8	13.4*
	* Significant at the 5% level				

TABLE 1. Average amount of borrowing by children of grammar and secondary modern standard.

number of books per child borrowed in a year. In Group 'A' are the children already in the grammar school or qualified to enter in the following year ; Group 'B' comprises children at or about to enter the secondary modern school.

In this sample, the children who are already at secondary schools borrow rather fewer library books than their counterparts still in the primary school, presumably because they have other things to occupy their time. In exception to this, the girls in the secondary modern school borrow slightly more on average than Group 'B' girls still in the primary school. These differences are not statistically significant, however, and in any case are less important than those between Group 'A' and Group 'B'. In every case there is a gap of roughly ten between the brighter and the weaker pupils, and between the two groups of primary girls the difference amounts to more than sixteen. The differences are smaller at the secondary stage, partly because the less assiduous readers among the secondary modern pupils have by now been winnowed out, and partly because the girls who enter the grammar tend to borrow rather fewer books than before.

All this accords with our previous evidence and is in keeping, too, with our expectation that the abler pupils should borrow more than others, if only because they are likely to be faster and more efficient readers. Moreover, their success at school tends to confirm for them the value of reading library books, and although in the grammar school the pressure of homework and perhaps the availability of other books often causes them to reduce their borrowing, few of them allow their membership to lapse, and, indeed, after entering the grammar school some join who have never joined before. Conversely, the less able pupils are likely to be less efficient readers and, in consequence, to borrow fewer books. Furthermore, in their case time spent in reading library books has brought no obvious benefit to their school-work. While this seems not to deter the girls at all, the boys' interest falters badly when they fail to reach the grammar school.

Educational Attainment and Standards of Difficulty

One obvious effect, then, of poor performance at school is to reduce the amount of reading a child does in its leisure time. In addition it affects the quality of the books chosen, above all, perhaps, in their level of difficulty : the books generally chosen by the abler pupils demand a considerably higher standard of reading ability than those chosen by the weaker pupils. As Table 2 shows, books chosen by children of grammar school standard include a higher proportion of books in Octavo format, have more pages, fewer illustrations, smaller type, and tend to be written in more difficult language.

	Boys			Girls		
	Group 'A'	Group 'B'	Diff.	Group 'A'	Group 'B'	Diff.
No. of Books	913	322		2,021	1,562	
% Octavo	95.1	91.5	3.6	97.1	92.5	4.6 **
Mean size of type	12.36	13.29	.93 **	13.26	14.24	.98 **
Mean no. of pages	206	187	19 **	205	181	24 **
% Illustration	3.9	9.5	5.6 **	3.8	6.8	3.0 **
Mean reading ease	71.8	76.0	4.2 **	74.5	77.0	2.5 **
		** Significant at the .1% level.				

TABLE 2.   External features of books issued to children of grammar and secondary modern standard.

The books chosen by the brighter boys have much the same external features as are characteristic of books chosen by the average boy of twelve, the less able boys, on the other hand, choose books of a similar order of difficulty to those chosen by boys at about the age of ten and a half. Among the girls, too, there is a difference roughly equivalent to eighteen months between the level of difficulty of books chosen by Group 'A' and by Group 'B'. There is reason to think, therefore, that in an unstreamed class of children aged eleven and twelve the books likely to be suitable for pupils in the upper half of the class will be advanced by about a year and a half in difficulty over those suited to the lower half.

It has often been suggested that in some respects girls are more mature in their reading tastes than boys. Differences there certainly are, but for teachers of mixed classes it is perhaps worth noting that in terms of difficulty the books chosen by the boys are if anything slightly superior to those chosen by girls of the same educational standard. To account for the very small differences that do appear, it must be borne in mind that the most backward among the boys rarely borrow books at all, whereas many quite retarded girls do so. Apart from that, the secondary modern boy tend to read a relatively high proportion of works of information, and these are often more difficult than works of fiction.

This illustrates an important point. If an interest in reading is to be encouraged, it is important that there should be a good supply of suitably easy books, but this is not the prime consideration. On the one hand, when reading for pleasure children as a rule choose books which are well within their capacity, but on the other, when they are especially interested in a topic, they often choose books which are unusually difficult. It happens that many of the less able boys are interested in practical subjects, and the fact that works of information are sometimes quite difficult to read does not deter them. The extent of a child's interest in the contents, then, is much more important than the level of difficulty of the book. Even so, it may well be that the poorer readers are unable to find books which are sufficiently simple on subjects which are of interest to them. The chief lack, one suspects, is of simply written works of information suited to the backward boy.

Education and Choice of Books

It is not altogether easy to explain why non-fiction bulks so large in the reading of the weaker boys. The weaker girls read non-fiction also, but as it consists largely of books of folk-lore which are akin to fairy stories, this is less surprising than the fact that the secondary modern boys should read so many books on science and the useful arts and crafts. It is possible that boys who do well at school, and especially those in the grammar school, use the public library solely for their fiction and find their ' serious ' reading elsewhere, but it is also possible that boys who are interested in fiction, and whose tastes are therefore essentially literary, tend to do better at school than those whose inclinations are more to practical subjects. At all events, boys who are more interested in non-fiction are not on the whole voracious readers, nor do they generally reach the grammar school. Can it be that boys who are successful in their dealings with books at school come to enjoy reading for its own sake and tend to read in their leisure time almost entirely for pleasure, whereas those whose experience of school books has not been so rewarding tend to read rather less for pleasure and rather more for profit ?

In the types of fiction that they choose, moreover, the brighter children differ substantially from the weaker, as Table 3 reveals.

Among the boys of grammar standard, Adventure Stories rank first in popularity, while Mystery Stories come second ; with the secondary modern boys this order is reversed, but with both groups the third place goes to Gang Stories. Together these three account for 83 per

	BOYS				GIRLS			
	Group 'A'	Group 'B'	Difference	Chi Square	Group 'A'	Group 'B'	Difference	Chi Square
Number of Books	976	413			2,066	1639		
	%	%	%		%	%	%	
Puppet	.3	2.2			.3	3.4		
Fairy	1.8	5.5			4.3	11.0		
Animal	3.6	2.4			2.0	2.9		
All Fantasy	5.7	10.1	—4.4	20.0	6.6	17.3	—10.7	102
Pony	.6	.2			4.8	6.0		
School	.5	.7			16.0	7.7		
Gang	14.7	11.4			15.0	10.0		
All Juvenile Realism	15.8	12.3	+3.5	2.2	35.8	23.7	+12.1	61
Mystery	20.2	38.0	—17.8	45.0	24.5	26.9		
Adventure	47.4	20.8	+26.6	87.5	4.8	6.5		
All Romance	67.6	58.8	+8.8	5.5	29.3	33.4	—4.1	5.9
Family	1.3	4.8			10.1	10.6		
Adolescent Novel	.5	.2			7.2	4.8		
Careers	.3	—			7.3	3.2		
All Adult Realism	2.1	5.0	—2.9	6.9	24.6	18.6	+6.0	15.9
Non-fiction	9.2	13.6	—4.4	5.2	3.2	6.5	—3.3	21

Note : Chi Square values greater than 3.84 are significant at the 5% level.

TABLE 3. Percentage of issues to children of Grammar and Secondary modern standard in each category.

cent of those issued to the former, for 70 per cent of those issued to the latter, and no other type of story holds a very strong appeal for either group. Among the girls, highest in favour with both grammar and secondary modern children come Mystery Stories, accounting for roughly a quarter of all issues in each case. Predictably enough, School Stories are more popular with the grammar than with the secondary modern pupils, ranking second with the former but in fourth place with the latter, while for Family Stories this order is reversed. With both groups Gang Stories hold third place. Together, these four kinds of stories account for 67 per cent of those borrowed by girls of grammar, and for 56 per cent by girls of secondary modern standard.

While there is a wide measure of over-lap between the tastes of the brighter and the weaker pupils, there are a number of differences pointing to the fact that the former are perceptibly more mature in their reading tastes. In the first place, the taste for Fantasy, though nearly out-grown, survives more strongly among the weaker pupils ; with them, Fairy Stories remain quite popular, and even Puppet Stories continue to be read in appreciable numbers by some girls at the secondary modern school. Conversely, they are relatively indifferent to realistic stories ; Pony Stories, Gang Stories and School Stories, which together make up the category we have called Juvenile Realism, are all more popular with the more successful pupils. Family Stories are more prominent among those issued to secondary modern than to grammar pupils, but significantly Careers Stories and Adolescent Novels, the other two belonging to the class of Adult Realism, are both more often borrowed by the brighter children.

The realism of the Family Story, the Careers Story and the Adolescent Novel appeals chiefly to girls, whereas boys are more given to reading romantic stories, the Mystery Story and the Adventure Story. It is noticeable, however, that of these two the Adventure Story with its grown-up characters, its unfamiliar settings and its atmosphere of violence appeals more to the brighter boys, while the Mystery Story with its young protagonists, its familiar settings and its holiday atmosphere appeals more strongly to the relatively backward boys. It is a curious fact, however, that both the Mystery and the Adventure Story are read more often by the weaker, rather than the brighter of the girls ; the latter, evidently, having long abandoned Fantasy, are already turning from Romance to the Adult Realism of the Careers

Story and the Adolescent Novel. One measure of this progress is the fact that, in 47 per cent of the books they choose, the characters are human beings portrayed in what we have defined as realistic terms, whereas this is the case in only 33 per cent of those chosen by girls of secondary modern standard. The boys, of course, are still in the romantic phase of reading : realistic characters appear in only 13 per cent of books read by boys of grammar standard and in 15 per cent by boys of secondary modern.

Yet more evidence of the relative maturity of the brighter children comes from an examination of the central characters in the books they choose. As they themselves grow older, children tend to identify themselves with progressively older characters, a clear sign of their growing readiness to face adult problems and of maturing reading tastes. In this sense, children of grammar school standard seem appreciably more advanced than those of secondary modern calibre. The former, at both the primary and the secondary stage, choose books the majority of which have heroes or heroines who are adolescents or adults, whereas the latter show a preference for tales with principal characters of pre-school or primary school age.

Table 4 gives the average age of the central character in the books chosen by grammar and secondary modern children respectively, and underlines the relative immaturity of the weaker pupils.

	Boys	Girls
Grammar Standard	14.3	12.9
Sec. Mod. Standard	12.2	12.0
Difference	2.1	.9
S. E. difference	.3	.15
Significance	$P < .001$	$P < .001$

TABLE 4.   Average age of main characters in books issued to grammar and secondary modern pupils.

There is reason to believe, moreover, that between the brighter and the weaker pupils the gap is wider at the secondary than at the primary stage, which suggests that those entering the grammar school mature more rapidly in their reading tastes than do those entering the secondary modern.

Reading Tastes and Measured Intelligence

The degree of success a child achieves at school is known to be linked with his intelligence as measured by tests of mental ability. We shall expect to find, therefore, between reading and intelligence, much the same sort of relationship as we have already found to exist between reading and educational attainment. However, there is some purpose in assessing separately the relationship with intelligence, if only because scores obtained in mental tests permit of finer gradings than simple success or failure in an examination, and, the test being standardised, afford a better basis of comparison between these and children living elsewhere.

It appears, not unexpectedly, that the more intelligent not only join the Library in greater numbers, but having joined, make more use of it than do the less intelligent. More surprising is the fact that on closer scrutiny the differences are extremely small. Among the boys, the correlation between intelligence and volume of reading (+.19) is not significantly greater than zero, and even among the girls is only marginally higher (+ .21 ; P< .05). It is clear, therefore, that the amount of reading a child does in his leisure time does not depend to any great extent upon his level of intelligence.

IQ	71—80	81—90	91—100	101—110	111—120	121+
Boys	17.0	15.4	19.1	22.1	15.2	41.7
Girls	36.0	27.8	30.2	30.1	33.9	39.6

TABLE 5.   Average number of books issued to children at each level of intelligence.

By and large, as may be seen from Table 5, the average rate of borrowing declines as the level of intelligence declines. To the extent that this occurs, it is due, no doubt, to the fact that reading ability is closely related to measured intelligence, and a child's rate of borrowing will depend to some extent upon the fluency with which he reads. This does not explain, however, why among the girls those with scores of 80 and below should read on average more than any other group except the most intelligent of all, and why among the boys those of similarly low intelligence also borrow at an unexpectedly high rate. When we consider separately those aged ten, eleven and twelve, the same anomaly appears to some degree among the boys and girls alike.

The evidence is not conclusive, but there are indications that the children who are most interested in reading tend to be found at the extremes of the scale of mental ability, among the very bright and the very dull, rather than among those whose intelligence is closer to the average. It may also prove to be the case that at the extremes of the scale of intelligence, the differences between boys and girls in the volume of their reading tend to disappear : in the present sample, it will be noticed, the brightest of the boys read quite as much as do the brightest of the girls.

This is a further pointer to the variety and complexity of the motives from which children read. A number of clues have already led us to suspect that in general boys and girls read for somewhat different reasons, the former for purposes not entirely divorced from their work at school, the latter more obviously for recreation. And now, finding that the very dull are almost as fervent in their reading as the very bright, we can only suppose that the satisfactions which they seek are not the same. It may help us to divine what their different purposes may be if we concentrate more narrowly upon the very bright and very dull.

The Brightest and Dullest Readers Compared

Table 6 permits us to compare the books issued to the five children with the highest intelligence scores (Mean 125) with those borrowed by the five at the very bottom of the scale (Mean 78). The over-all impression given is that the books chosen by the very bright are considerably more difficult than the choices of the very dull. Among the former there is a higher proportion of books in Octavo format, they have more pages and fewer illustrations, the print is smaller and the language more difficult to read. Nearly all the differences are statistically highly significant ; the more surprising of the two exceptions draws attention to the low score for Reading Ease among the books borrowed by the girls of high intelligence. The fact that in terms of Reading Ease the gap between the very bright and very dull is so narrow suggests that the more intelligent of the girls often read in their leisure books which make small demands upon their reading ability or their mental powers. At the other end of the scale, one supposes, children of very low intelligence find their capacities strained to the utmost by the effort of reading books appropriate to their level of emotional development.

	Boys			Girls		
	High IQ	Low IQ	Diff.	High IQ	Low IQ	Diff.
No. of Books	222	142		229	129	
% Octavo	99	89	+10**	96	79	+17**
Mean size of Type	13.3	13.9	—.6	13.2	17.3	—4.1**
Mean no. of Pages	208	182	+26**	190	124	+66**
Mean % Illustration	3.4	9.7	—6.3**	6.1	19.6	—13.5**
Mean Reading Ease	72.1	78.3	—6.2**	77.5	79.8	—2.3
		**	Significant at the .1% level			

TABLE 6. Analysis of books issued to the five most intelligent and the five least intelligent among the eleven-year-old readers.

To some extent, the choices which children make may not reflect accurately their real tastes and interests, but may be forced on them by the absence of books which are suitable both in language and in content. It may well be that those responsible for producing children's books, in trying to cater for the majority, neglect the minority at each end of the scale. As a result, there may be a lack of books for the highly intelligent, dealing with themes in which they are interested in language which offers a real challenge to their intelligence, and on the other hand a shortage of books designed for children of limited ability, treating subjects suited to their age and interests in language within the scope of their understanding. For the least able, in any case, the effective range of choice is much narrower than for abler children, since books written in language too difficult for them to read are to all intents and purposes inaccessible to them.

However, the choices of the very bright and very dull differ in ways which cannot be accounted for entirely in this way. In terms of difficulty, as we have seen, the gap between the two is sometimes very narrow ; in themes and treatment, nevertheless, the books they borrow differ markedly, and these divergences result not so much from differences in powers of understanding as from different tastes and attitudes to reading. It is also true, however, that between the brightest and the dullest girls the differences in reading tastes are wider than between the boys : the broad conclusion seems to be that girls of low

	Boys			Girls		
	High IQ	Low IQ	Diff.	High IQ	Low IQ	Diff.
	%	%	%	%	%	%
Puppet	—	.7	—.7	—	17.0	—17.0***
Fair	.5	7.7	—7.2**	6.7	27.8	—21.1***
Animal	6.8	2.1	+4.7*	1.3	9.3	—8.0**
All Fantasy	7.2	10.5	—3.3	8.0	54.2	—46.2***
Pony	—	—	—	1.3	.8	+ .5
School	.5	1.4	—.9	12.6	—	+12.6**
Gang	14.4	16.1	—1.7	15.1	9.3	+5.8
All Juvenile Realism	14.9	17.5	—2.6	29.0	10.1	+18.9***
Mystery	24.8	37.3	—12.5**	34.7	8.5	+26.2***
Adventure	45.9	18.9	—27.0***	2.5	6.2	—3.7
All Romance	70.7	56.2	+14.5**	37.2	14.7	+22.5***
Family	.5	4.9	—4.4*	15.2	6.2	+8.9*
Adolescent Novel	—	—	—	2.5	—	+2.5
Careers	.5	—	+ .5	6.2	.8	+5.4
All Adult Realism	1.0	4.9	— 3.9	23.8	7.0	+16.8***
Non-Fiction	6.3	10.5	—4.2	2.1	14.0	—11.9***

*   Significant at the 5% level.
** Significant at the 1% level.
*** Significant at the .1% level.

TABLE 7.   Analysis of books issued to the five most intelligent and the five least intelligent among the eleven-year-old readers, showing the percentage in each category.

intelligence are almost equally as keen to join the Library as those of higher intelligence, but having joined they tend to choose vastly different books ; the less intelligent among the boys, on the other hand, join the Library comparatively seldom, but having done so tend to read much the same kinds of books as do the abler boys.

Between the bright and the dull there are certain differences which are common to both boys and girls. Table 7 reveals once more the odd fact that relatively few works of non-fiction are borrowed by the most intelligent ; on the contrary, the keenest readers of factual books appear to be children of quite limited intelligence. Paradoxical as it may seem, the duller readers also have the strongest inclination to read Fantasy : nearly all the Puppet and Fairy Stories issued to boys aged eleven or more are borrowed by those with an intelligence score of 80 and below, while these two types together account for nearly a half of the books borrowed by girls of this standard of intelligence. At first sight it is not easy to explain why children who evidently like factual works should at the same time so much enjoy the patent un-reality of the Puppet and the Fairy Story, but on reflection it appears that these children, the girls especially, tend to avoid what may be called 'human' fiction—fiction, that is, which deals with human beings and has some claim to verisimilitude. The attitude of these children, were they able to put it into words, seems to be that they like their facts to be obviously true and their fiction to be obviously false, and that they prefer to avoid the twilight zone between.

At the other extreme, what distinguishes the most intelligent is their appetite for 'human' fiction. Fantasy and Non-fiction together account for only ten per cent of the issues to the brightest girls ; ninety per cent are stories, realistic or romantic, dealing with human beings and human experience, whereas books of this kind form less than a third of those chosen by girls at the bottom of the scale. Among the boys the contrast is less marked, but it is again evident that the appetite for ordinary fiction is stronger in the most intelligent.

There are other differences which cannot be explained in quite these terms. It is not difficult to understand why girls of low intelligence should read none of the School Stories which are popular with others of their age, but it is less obvious why they choose so very few of the Mystery Stories which are so widely read, not only by the majority of girls of eleven and twelve, but also by boys no more intelligent than themselves. Equally odd is the fact that, compared with the majority of their sex, the least intelligent boys read more Gang Stories and Family Stories, while the least intelligent girls read fewer.

The child of average intelligence or more may be supposed to cope fairly adequately with the situations confronting him in the physical world and in the sphere of human relations. To that extent he is free to send his imagination forward, as it were, to reconnoitre the life that lies ahead, and much of his reading therefore becomes a form of preparation for the future. As we have seen, the average child tends to choose books which are set in scenes as yet unknown to him, among people older than himself and engaged in activities to which he has not yet been initiated ; he often seeks to model himself on characters more mature than himself, possessing qualities and attributes to which as yet he can only aspire. On the other hand, the child of very low intelligence is, almost by definition, one who finds difficulty in dealing with situations which his age-mates meet with ease : whereas they adapt themselves quickly to the physical and social world in which they find themselves, he is anxious and perplexed. Two courses are open to a child so handicapped : on the one hand he may redouble his efforts to comprehend his situation or, on the other, he may refuse to meet reality. As far as their reading is concerned, those who adopt the first course will tend to choose books which have some relevance to their immediate problems and their day-to-day experience—School Stories, Gang Stories and Family Stories which deal realistically with their own kind of life ; those who adopt the second will turn to the Puppet and the Fairy Stories which enable them to regress in imagination to a simpler world and a more immediately satisfying mode of life. The dullest of the boys here considered seem on the whole to have adopted the former course ; the dullest of the girls appear to be committed to the second.

More than one third of the books chosen by the average boy of eleven or twelve are set against unfamiliar back-grounds—in the desert, jungle, in great cities or in foreign countries—and the most intelligent among them evince an even stronger liking for these remote and exotic scenes. The least intelligent, in contrast, choose roughly only half that proportion of books with such settings, and tend more to favour books set against the familiar back-ground of the country-side, the village or small town. Far from avoiding stories set in school, they read as many of them as do the most intelligent, but are less interested than the brighter boys in tales of high adventure, war, capture and escape, violent crime and death. They turn instead to books such as those of Richmal Crompton and Arthur Ransome, and to Mystery Stories such as those of Enid Blyton, all of which deal essentially with the activities of children like themselves, with boyish sport and mischief, and the rivalries and friendships of the peer group. The heroes they adopt are not the men or youths of courage, aggressiveness and powers of leadership admired by other boys, but children more of their own age who, by dint of loyalty to their companions, win acceptance among other boys and girls, in the family, and in the community at large.

	High IQ	Low IQ	Diff.
Boys	14.0	11.2	2.8*
Girls	12.0	9.3	2.7
	* Significant at the .1% level		

TABLE 8. Average age of heroes and heroines in books borrowed by the five most intelligent and five least intelligent among the eleven-year-olds.

In certain aspects, it is true, the books chosen by boys of low intelligence are very similar to those favoured by rather younger children, and in that sense these boys tend to be immature in their reading. In its total pattern, however, their reading differs not only from that of the average boy of their own age, but from that of younger children also. It is not that the dull eleven-year-old reads like a boy of nine, though in certain superficial respects this is obviously true. The fact is that he reads for a quite different purpose, as an eleven-year-old striving to be accepted as an eleven-year-old. Others of his age read to anticipate the future ; he reads to meet and comprehend the present.

The same cannot be said of the least intelligent among the girls. The books they choose bear many of the hall-marks of those read by girls two or three years younger than themselves : nearly a fifth of the stories they read are set in fairy-land or in the world of magic, and a further fifteen per cent in domestic settings—the nursery, home or farm. To point the contrast, the proportions for the brightest girls among the eleven-year-olds are 4 per cent and 7 per cent respectively, and for the age-group as a whole 7 per cent and 6 per cent. Were this all, they might be thought merely immature in their reading. At the same time, however, 20 per cent of their stories—proportionately twice as many as are chosen by the very bright—have romantic or exotic back-grounds such as jungles, deserts and foreign cities ; they entirely shun stories in school settings, and are relatively uninterested in stories against the familiar back-cloth of the country-side or village. All this goes to suggest that these girls read neither to prepare for an advance to new experience nor to deal more effectively with their present situation, but to find a refuge from their every-day existence. This is borne out by their lack of interest in books which deal with human beings. More than half the stories they read are peopled by toys, fairies or animals, and when they read of human beings, they prefer them to be portrayed in romantic rather than in realistic terms. Their choice of themes reveals the same desire for escape : they show little interest in the activities of children like themselves, in relationships between members of a family or with friends, but are drawn more to tales of fantasy or magic, to stories of extravagant humour or sensational adventure. Most significant of all is their reluctance to identify themselves with characters of their own age and sex. The average age of the main characters in the books they choose is only 9.3. That this is not statistically significant is due simply to the fact that only in a comparatively small proportion of their books is there a human character at all.

What needs to be emphasised is that this is indicative not only of an immaturity which might be expected to remedy itself as the child grows up, but also of a regression to infancy and a withdrawal from reality which might conceivably impede the child's social and emotional development. To judge by their reading, the majority of girls of eleven and twelve attach great value to gregariousness : the attribute which more than any other distinguishes the heroes and heroines they admire is that of loyalty to, and acceptance by, their fellows. The girls of limited intelligence seem conspicuously indifferent to such qualities ; their favourite characters are often solitary individuals, secure in their enjoyment of parental protection, or possessed of a magic secret which will grant them all their wishes. In this respect, they contrast sharply with the boys of similar intelligence, who, to judge from the books they read, value the companionship of their peers even more than do most other boys. Whereas it seems to be the boys' ideal to be as much like other boys as possible, these girls appear to want, not to be like other girls, but to escape from themselves and be quite other than they are.

Turning to children at the opposite extreme, we find that children ot very high intelligence are not outstandingly more mature in their reading than others of their age. In most respects, perhaps, the interests of very bright eleven-year-olds, for instance, are closer to those of boys and girls aged twelve than to those of their own age, but in no sense are the books they choose as far superior as their mental age seems to permit. The fact is that in experience, in first-hand knowledge of human vicissitudes and relationships, they are not necessarily less limited than their fellows, and it is this, rather than their mental ability, which determines the sort of subjects which will interest them in books. Broadly speaking, then, the choices of highly intelligent readers are not startlingly different from those of the average boy or girl, and such differences as do appear do not suggest that these children differ radically from the majority in their approach and attitude to reading.

The example of the eleven-year-olds will perhaps illustrate these points. Long before this age, as we have seen, boys begin to turn from the Puppet and the Fairy Story, first to the Mystery, and later still increasingly to the Adventure Story. This, roughly, is the path they follow in their progress towards mature reading tastes, and it appears that on this path the most intelligent eleven-year-olds are ahead of the majority of that age, but still some way behind the average boy of twelve. Mystery and Adventure Stories respectively account for 25 per cent and 46 per cent of the books issued to the most intelligent (IQ 120+) eleven-year-olds, while the corresponding figures for the average boy of twelve are 18 per cent and 49 per cent. To compare the average ages of the heroes they admire brings out the point even more clearly perhaps : in books issued to all eleven-year-olds, the average is 13.2 years ; to all twelve-year-olds, 15.0 ; to the most intelligent of the eleven-year-olds, 14.0. In general, then, the reading tastes of the brightest boys at eleven fall some way between those of the average eleven-year-old and those of twelve-year-olds. The differences between them and their age-mates are smaller than might have been expected, but the direction of these differences is much what might have been anticipated. They show remarkably little interest in stories set against prosaic or familiar backgrounds : the home, the school, the country-side, the village and the small town are much less attractive to them than to their age-mates, and they read instead stories about places associated with freedom and adventure. A remarkable number of the books they choose have a holiday back-ground—the sea-side, castles, caves and so on—and, of course, many others are stories about the sea, the air, foreign lands and distant planets. Even more than boys of average intelligence, these boys appear to find their every-day existence too restricted, and read not so much to explore their present situation as to transcend its narrow limits.

The girls of high intelligence differ from their age-mates even less, if anything, than do the boys. They read fewer works of Fantasy than do the majority of the same age, but their choices among books reveal few other signs of exceptional maturity. There are even signs of a certain immaturity, notably in their lack of interest in stories in which adults are involved. On approaching adolescence, girls become increasingly concerned with their relations with grown-ups, and this is reflected in their growing fondness for Adventure Stories, Adolescent Novels and Careers Stories. At the age of eleven or twelve, however, the highly intelligent girl is not conspicuously more interested than the average girl in stories of this sort. On the contrary, she appears to read more Mystery Stories than the average girl, and, since the characters in these are predominantly children, the impression her reading gives is of a child entirely absorbed in the affairs of childhood. The average age of the main characters in the books the bright eleven-year-old girls choose is 12.0 years, certainly higher than the 11.7 which is the average for the age-group as a whole, but low in comparison with the 13.0 which is the average for twelve-year-olds. Moreover, their reading is confined, to an unexpected degree, to books which have as their back-ground places such as are probably quite familiar to them : the school, the country-side and the sea-side appear surprisingly often, while remote or foreign settings are correspondingly rare. In short, their reading expresses none of the yearning for wider horizons, none of the longing for grown-up freedom which seem to inspire the reading of boys of similarly high intelligence at this age. On the contrary, the holiday atmosphere so prevalent in their stories, the youthfulness of the characters, and above all, perhaps, their liking for easy reading, all point to the conclusion that for girls of high intelligence the reading of library books is essentially a form of relaxation, almost of self-indulgence, and as such quite different from the "serious" reading they associate with school.

In conclusion, then, it appears that a child's reading interests do depend to some extent upon his level of intelligence. This does not mean, however, that he reads at a level of maturity corresponding to his mental age. On the contrary, as we have seen, in terms of maturity, the very bright are not outstandingly superior to their age-mates. Instead, it appears that on the one hand the very bright, and on the other, the very dull, have their own characteristic attitude to reading which is quite different from that of children of average intelligence. This, however, is a question to which we shall return in a later chapter.

CHAPTER VIII

HOME BACK-GROUND AND READING INTERESTS

WITH whatever aspect of human behaviour we may be concerned, it is always difficult to disentangle the effects upon it of innate potential, physical environment and cultural influences. We have already considered to what extent and in what ways children's reading tastes and habits are affected by their educational attainment and level of intelligence, but it will be conceded that other, possibly more important, factors are involved. The home, it will hardly be denied, plays an important part in laying the foundation of reading skills and in fostering an interest in books. Some children, at least, are taught to read and acquire a taste for books long before they enter school, and it is not unknown for some to be brought to the Library to choose their books even at the age of three. All children are not so fortunate, however, and it appears at first sight that both materially and culturally the advantages are with children who come from middle-class homes. The more prosperous the home, the more able will it be to afford the warmth, light and privacy which are necessary if much time is to be spent in reading, and the more likely it is to contain an adequate supply of books and other reading matter. Furthermore, in all probability the family is small and the children in it relatively free from the task of looking after younger children and from other house-hold chores. All this means that physical conditions in the middle-class home will generally be more favourable to reading, but to these must be added other less tangible advantages. The parents are likely to be more intelligent and better educated than parents who do manual work. Their children benefit from this in many ways : they tend to inherit their parents' high intelligence ;[1] they are more likely to be given a grammar school education ;[2] by dint of hearing and using language of good quality in the home, they are better able to acquire verbal skills[3] ; and their parents are more likely to encourage them by

[1]See, for example, Thorndike (1951).
[2]Douglas (1964) pp. 14—22.
[3]Bernstein (1961).

precept and example, not only in reading, but in all their work at school.[1] Moreover, the neighbourhood in which the home is set tends to re-inforce the influence of the home itself. The middle-class home usually forms part of a community in which the material and cultural standards are generally high, whereas the manual worker's home not infrequently belongs to an area ill-supplied with schools, libraries and other such amenities, where the language is often impoverished and incorrect, and where an interest in books, so far from being taken for granted, may well be looked upon askance.

In view of these supposed advantages, it may be asked, does the middle-class child make more use of the Library than other children ? Are the books he chooses more difficult and more demanding ? Are his reading tastes, as reflected in the kind of books he chooses, different from, more mature or more cultivated than, those of children from manual workers' homes ? In order to find answers to these questions, we need to compare the middle-class children with others of the same age, sex and level of intelligence from a different socio-economic back-ground. Taking the eleven-year-olds as a convenient age-cohort, we may divide those of each sex into four groups : Group I, consisting of children with an intelligence score of 100 or more, and whose parents are in non-manual occupations ; Group II, those children also above average in intelligence scores, but whose parents are in manual occupations ; Group III, consisting of children with intelligence below 100 and whose parents are non-manual workers ; Group IV, children who also have intelligence scores below the average, but whose parents are manual workers. The task, in essence, is to compare the reading habits of Group I with those of Group II, and those of Group III with Group IV.

Social Class and Volume of Borrowing

In Chapter VI, we found no reason to believe that the children of manual workers were any less likely to use the Library than those of non-manual parents, and there is no reason now for revising this conclusion. Moreover, when we consider the number of books borrowed, we find that the differences between individuals in the same group far outweigh those between the various groups, and in

---

[1]Coster (1958).

any case the differences between the social classes are much smaller than those between children of different levels of intelligence.

	Group I	Group II	Group III	Group IV
Boys				
No. in Group	21	25	10	38
Readers %	52	48	30	47
Average issues per reader	26.6	20.0	19.7	11.7
Standard deviation	23.7	14.5	6.6	14.5
Girls				
No. in Group	17	23	9	42
Readers %	76	83	78	76
Average issues per reader	32.2	31.0	47.1	20.3
Standard deviation	19.9	20.9	51.1	11.7

TABLE 1. Membership and rate of borrowings among eleven-year-olds, according to intelligence and social class.

Note : None of the differences between Groups I and II, or between Groups III and IV, are statistically significant.

Nor, turning to our second question, have we found any reason to believe that children from middle-class homes customarily choose more difficult and demanding books than do children of the same level of intelligence from a different back-ground. In their external features —their format, number of pages, proportion of pictures, size of type and score for Reading Ease, the books issued to Group I do not differ significantly from those borrowed by Group II, nor those chosen by Group III from those of Group IV. There is little warrant, therefore, for supposing that home influences have any appreciable effect upon the level of difficulty at which children read, nor, perhaps, is this surprising when we remember that children rarely choose, for their leisure reading, the most difficult books they are capable of understanding. The influence of the home, therefore, will tend to be reflected more in the contents of the books which children choose, rather than in their readability.

Reading Interests and Parental Occupation—Boys

We turn, therefore, to our third question : Do the tastes of children from middle-class homes differ significantly from those of the children from manual workers' homes ? That is to say, are the books issued to the former drawn from substantially the same categories as those issued to the latter. It will be as well for us to consider separately the borrowings of children of above average and below average intelligence.

BOYS

	Group I % (N=294)	Group II % (N=240)	Difference	Chi Square	Significance
Fantasy Juvenile	7.8	6.3	+1.5	.42	N.S.
Realism	18.0	10.0	+8.0	5.26	P<.05
Mystery	31.3	24.6	+6.7	2.17	N.S.
Adventure Adult	29.4	40.8	−11.4	4.89	P<.05
Realism	2.7	4.2	−1.5	.90	N.S.
Non-Fiction	10.5	14.2	−3.7	1.49	N.S.

TABLE 2. Percentage in each category of books issued to boys of above average intelligence from manual and non-manual homes.

It is evident from Table 2 that the books issued to boys in Group I belong substantially to the same categories as those borrowed by Group II. In both groups, the Gang Story, the Mystery and the Adventure together account for the vast bulk of all those chosen. The Gang Story, however, is more prominent among those chosen by boys from non-manual homes, while the Adventure Story forms a significantly larger proportion of those issued to boys from manual workers' homes. This contrast of attitudes towards the Gang Story and the Adventure Story seems clearly to reflect differences in social back-ground and cultural values. Typically, the world of the Gang Story is a middle-class world : its main characters are usually the sons and daughter of the well-to-do, and bear the obvious signs of a privileged up-bringing—cultured speech and easy manners, private chools and expensive holidays. More significantly, perhaps, there is a tacit acceptance in almost all these stories of middle-class values and conventions—the respect for property, for rank, for non-manual work, for a settled and ordered way of life. Equally clearly, the Adventure Story rejects this ideal in favour of what is perhaps the older one of the pioneer, the outlaw and the warrior. The home, it is clear, rarely influences directly its children's choice of books. Rather is it that a child's reading reflects his acceptance or rejection of the values that prevail in it. Thus, in their fondness for the Gang Story, these middle-class boys appear to be expressing their contentment with their middle-class way of life, while the working-class boys, inevitably perhaps, will be less disposed to favour a kind of book which exemplifies values in many ways at variance with those prevailing in their homes. To the latter the Adventure Story with its insistence upon physical prowess makes a much more obvious appeal.

When we compare the books issued to Groups III and IV, however, we find what appears to be a flat contradiction. Among boys of less than average intelligence, those from middle-class homes are far more addicted to Adventure Stories than those of the working class, whereas the Mystery Story bulks very large among the issues to the latter.

Boys

	Group III % (N = 57)	Group IV % (N = 269)	Difference	Chi Square	Significance
Fantasy	5.3	6.1	−.8	0	N.S.
Juvenile Realism	15.8	8.0	+7.8	2.83	N.S.
Mystery	7.0	46.2	−39.2	18.2	P <.001
Adventure	42.1	20.7	+21.4	8.12	P <.01
Adult Realism	7.0	3.8	+3.2	1.14	N.S.
Non-Fiction	22.8	15.1	+7.7	1.63	N.S.

TABLE 3. Percentage in each category of books issued to boys below average intelligence from manual and non-manual homes.

This effectively disposes of any suggestion that children's reading tastes are determined in any rigid or direct fashion by environmental factors. It is a reminder that the individual is not inert under the impress of external pressures ; his native attributes and capacities may render him singularly apt to receive their imprint or remarkably resistant. One may imagine, therefore, two boys from middle-class homes, the one intelligent and successful at school, the other not. The first may be thought of as acquiescing happily to the pressures upon him to accept middle-class values and the middle-class way of life ; the second, feeling himself to have little aptitude for the academic success upon which his parents set such store and which is the pass-port to the middle-class way of life, rejects these values, and gives expression to his revolt through his fondness for the Adventure Story. At the same time, it is easy to imagine that for the working-class boy of good intelligence there may be a certain conflict between the basic values of the school and of the home. In a sense, he belongs to two worlds and is the focus of conflicting codes, loyalties and aspirations. His very success at school threatens to separate him from his parents, from his brothers even, and from other children with a similar social back-ground. Because he is good at school, he expects and is expected to give more time to reading than to the out-door activities in which his age-mates join. Others enjoy already a large measure of physical freedom, and can look forward to an early release from school and even greater independence in the near future ; for him, on the other hand, school and school work fill the whole horizon, and beyond it lies the prospect, not of a life of physical effort which, because it is his father's, he feels is proper to a man, but of another, less active and less manly way of life. His reading seems to crystallise his dilemma : were he less competent at school work, he would not read so much ; were a life of physical effort and strenuous activity not attractive, he would not choose Adventure Stories. Finally, the boy of less than average intelligence from the manual worker's home chiefly enjoys Mystery Stories ; his satisfaction stems from the vicarious experience they offer of the companionship of other children and for the compensation they afford for the disparagement he has known from adults.

Reading Interests and Parental Occupation—Girls

Whereas boys at this age tend to restrict their choices to books belonging to a single category or at most to two or three, girls tend to be more catholic in their tastes ; each reader may choose a different type of book from week to week or day to day, in response to the mood of the moment rather than to any single, more abiding need.

Since each girl tends to read from every category impartially, the differences between one girl and another are usually less clear-cut than is the case with boys, with the result that between groups of readers from each of the two social classes the differences are never as large as the largest found among the boys.

Mystery Stories form the largest class among the books issued to every group except Group IV, for whom works of Fantasy take pride of place. What we have called Juvenile Realism—the Pony Story, the School Story and the Gang Story together—accounts for almost as many, and is equally popular with all groups except, again, Group IV. Puppet Stories, Fairy Stories and Animal Stories bulk much larger among the issues to the less intelligent and tend also to be chosen more often by girls from manual workers' homes, as do works of information.

Considering first the books chosen by the girls of more than average intelligence, we find very few differences between the borrowings of the middle-class and of the working-class children. Works of Fantasy and works of information form a significantly higher proportion of the latter, but no other category is appreciably more attractive to one group than to the other. It was suggested in an earlier chapter that a liking for Fantasy and Non-fiction together reflects a certain lack of interest in ' human ' fiction, and may reflect a certain desire to retreat from reality.

GIRLS

	Group I % (N=418)	Group II % (N=589)	Difference	Chi Square	Significance
Fantasy	8.1	12.2	—4.1	3.88	P<.05
Juvenile Realism	30.6	26.8	+3.8	1.17	N.S.
Mystery	30.9	29.7	+1.2	.04	N.S.
Adventure	5.3	4.4	+ .9	.34	N.S.
Adult Realism	22.3	20.9	+1.4	.17	N.S.
Non-Fiction	2.9	5.9	—3.0	4.92	P<.05

TABLE 4.   Percentage in each category of books issued to girls of above average intelligence from manual and non-manual homes.

It seems, at all events, that the middle-class girls tend to favour more realistic fiction, and this leads one to suppose that they are less dissatisfied with life as they know it than are girls from manual workers' homes.

Between Groups III and IV the differences are more pronounced. Nearly all are large enough to be statistically significant, and together they clearly reflect a sharp contrast in attitudes towards reading. The girls from non-manual homes are chiefly interested in stories about children. The Pony, School and Gang Stories, the Mystery and the Family Stories, all of which bulk larger in their choices than among those chosen by girls from manual working class homes, have this in common, that they deal with the activities of children of about their own age. It is most noticeable that, in contrast, the books issued to girls in Group IV are peopled by characters quite different from their readers and are set against back-grounds which contrast strongly with their readers' own environment. In some ways, the choices made by girls in Group IV betray a certain immaturity : the Puppet, Fairy and Animal Stories prominent among them are most commonly chosen by the very young. Their fondness for the Adventure Story, however, points in the opposite direction. The total pattern of their reading, therefore, strongly suggests that these children do not read primarily to comprehend their immediate predicament but to find refuge from it.

GIRLS

	Group III % (N=330)	Group IV % (N=650)	Difference	Chi Square	Significance
Fantasy	22.8	27.8	—5.0	2.52	N.S.
Juvenile Realism	26.1	19.1	+7.0	4.78	P <.05
Mystery	27.0	19.7	+7.3	4.14	P <.05
Adventure	3.9	8.1	—4.2	5.54	P <.05
Adult Realism	17.6	16.0	+1.6	.24	N.S.
Non-Fiction	3.0	9.2	—6.2	12.42	P <.001

TABLE 5.   Percentage in each category of books issued to girls of below average intelligence from manual and non-manual homes.

Again, it is interesting to speculate as to why the Mystery Story should be more attractive to girls of the Non-manual than of the Manual working class. We have suggested that the Mystery Story responds to the child's desire to penetrate the secrecy which, as it seems to him, much of the behaviour of grown-ups is deliberately shrouded, and at the same time allows him vicariously to turn the tables on the adult society to which he is in subjection. One is tempted to think—with how much justice is uncertain—that in comparison with working-class girls those of the middle class are subjected to much narrower control and supervision, but that in spite of being more confined to the home they have no great share in managing the household, and rarely, therefore, have any sense of equality or partnership with their mothers. Undoubtedly the contrast here is over-drawn, but since the working-class family is often larger, the home more crowded, household work much greater, and the struggle to make ends meet more obvious, it is reasonable to think that the working-class girl generally suffers less from the over-solicitude of parents, that she is more aware of her parents' anxieties and problems and is more often called upon to share her mother's work. Studies of working-class life such as those of Hoggart (1957) and of Young and Wilmott (1957) stress the enduring strength of the bond between the working-class mother and her daughter, the origins of which would seem to lie in the circumstances which make intimacy and co-operation between mother and young daughter almost a necessity in the poorer home. And this, perhaps, is why these girls show relatively little interest in the Mystery Story : they do not share the middle-class child's sense of being over-protected and of being excluded from the grown-up world, and in consequence have less need for the type of compensation this kind of story appears to afford.

Conclusions

In the fore-going pages we have tried to discover how books issued to children from middle-class homes differ from those borrowed by children lower in the social scale. We have also speculated, going well beyond our evidence, it may be thought, upon the motives which may underlie these apparent differences in taste. It must be admitted that the evidence we offer affords scant basis for wide generalisations since the number of children in each group, and especially among the less intelligent from non-manual homes, is rather small, although the total number of acts of choice is reasonably large. However, it may be as well now to summarise our conclusions.

There is no reason to suppose that children from manual workers' homes are less eager to join the library than others of the same level of intelligence from non-manual homes, nor does it appear that the latter take out more books. It cannot be doubted that the middle-class children have better opportunities for reading and receive more encouragement to develop an interest in books, and it may well be that if books from other sources were included, the middle-class children would be found to read much more than children from homes lower in the social scale, for whom, in many cases, the Public Library may be the only source of books. Certainly, were the home to remain the sole or dominating influence in children's lives, the advantages to the middle-class child would be over-whelming. However, by the age of eleven, at least, since working-class children are not appreciably less interested in library books than other children, we may judge that the provision of public libraries and common schooling has gone some way to redress the balance.

In the types of books which interest them, however, children from contrasting back-grounds differ rather more, but we must guard against assuming a one-to-one relationship between a child's home circumstances and the kind of books he reads. Environmental factors may be thought to influence children in their choice of books in two main ways. In the first place, the home may be regarded as exercising a direct effect upon the reader, influencing him by precept and example to choose certain books and subjects, and to avoid others, pre-disposing him to admire certain modes of behaviour and certain personal attributes on the part of fictional characters, and to reject others. That is to say, the young reader might be expected to apply to his evaluation of people and events in books a scale of values which he has acquired in the home and which is prevalent in the social class to which he belongs. But the child's environment may be regarded as having another, much less direct, bearing on his choice of books. His home, with the material conditions it provides, the opportunities it offers, the standards it assumes, and the expectations it holds, presents the child with a series of complex problems of adjustment with which he copes with varying degrees of competence. From this standpoint, what is important is not the home back-ground in itself so much as the child's reaction to that environment, the degree to which in it he is happy or unhappy, successful or unsuccessful, frustrated or fulfilled. Conceivably, therefore, a child's choice of books might reflect directly the tastes and cultural standards with which he is familiar in the home, or in a more oblique and perhaps symbolic fashion express his inward response to this environment.

We have found little that suggests that the direct influences are very great. The Gang Story, with its essentially middle-class *milieu*, appeals more to non-manual children, but there is nothing that is distinctively 'working-class' about the books chosen by children of manual workers : their heroes, for example, are not noticeably more plebeian, nor are their settings in any way less *bourgeois* than in the books chosen by other children. We do not know whether or not middle-class parents make more effort than working-class parents to supervise their children's reading at this age,[1] but we can say that if in fact they do make any greater effort it has no very obvious results. We can dismiss out of hand the notion that working-class children are in some way cruder or less cultivated in their reading tastes than other children. It is worth stressing this point because much of the recent work done on class attitudes and sub-cultures has, although inadvertently, given renewed currency to old stereotyped conceptions of social differences, and may have lent new colour to the idea that members of the working class tend, in one way or another, to be more earthy than others.

At the same time, the reader can no more be indifferent to his social back-ground than to any other important facet of his environment. But it is his attitude to his back-ground, rather than the back-ground itself, which is reflected in his reading. It may be useful here to distinguish, as certain sociologists[2] have done in another context, the upwardly mobile, the downwardly mobile, and the socially static, members of each class, and to regard the intelligent working-class child as upwardly mobile, in a sense, the middle-class child of low intelligence as downwardly mobile, the intelligent middle-class child and the unintelligent working-class child as both socially static. We may put it less pretentiously, perhaps, and speak of middle-class

---

[1]Brearley (1949) claims to have found no evidence that parents in "better-class" homes exercise more supervision than others over their children's reading. p. 91.

[2]Havighurst (1961) ; Marsden and Jackson (1962).

children who are complacent or disgruntled, and of working-class children who are aspiring or resigned. It is not difficult to detect, beneath the taste for violent adventure which characterises the less intelligent of the middle-class boys, an unconscious rejection of middle-class standards, under the fondness for the Gang Story which the brighter middle-class boys show, their unquestioning acceptance of that way of life ; we may sense, too, the feeling of inadequacy which prompts the working-class girl of low intelligence to turn away from any book which reminds her of reality. At the same time, none of these attitudes to reading is peculiar to children of one social class : rebellious children are to be found in all walks of life, as are the ambitious, the complacent and the resigned, and in every social class there will be children who read for escape, for compensation, for some form of wish-fulfilment, or, quite uncomplicatedly, for relaxation. What must be stressed is that a child's reading can be understood only as part of his total effort to come to terms with his environment, of which, self-evidently, his home and social circumstances are important elements.

Other Environmental Factors

Homes differ from one another, in any case, in many other ways than the purely socio-economic ; the material comforts that the home affords and the conventional standards it reflects depend, no doubt, to a large degree upon the occupational status and class allegiance of the parents, but whether it provides its members with a stable, happy and stimulating environment depends on other, more intangible and less measurable, factors. The sense of insecurity which results from a broken home, for instance, is known to have far-reaching effects upon a child, and it is highly likely that an unstable back-ground of this kind will profoundly affect the needs which a child seeks to satisfy through reading. Will children who are deprived in this way tend to regard books as offering some form of compensation ? Will they be more addicted to reading than are other children ? Are they prone to choose books which in some way give them a vicarious experience of security ?[1] To these questions there are as yet no answers.

---

[1]Wollner (1949, p. 74), though not directly dealing with the broken home, claims that emotional deprivation sometimes manifests itself in voracious, haphazard and undiscriminating reading.

Moreover, we cannot ignore the part played in a child's experience of family life by the other children in it. It is likely, as has already been suggested, that a child has less time and less inclination for reading when there are others in the family with whom to share his leisure. Much more interesting, but much more difficult to estimate, are the possible effects upon the child's motives for reading and his preferences among books. It may help us to form a clearer idea of what these effects might be to compare the situation of the only child with that of the child who is a member of what the Crowther Report terms an ' all-through ' family. The extended family of Victorian times, which united under the same roof relatives of many generations and degrees of kinship, has become a rarity in our day, but in its modern equivalent, the ' all-through ' family which includes, in addition to the parents, members of either sex spanning a wide range of ages, the child's experience of domestic life is quite different from that of the child in a small family. The former kind of home, as the Crowther Report points out, acts as a school for personal responsibility and informal education in which the growing child has opportunities to learn of birth, death, courtship and marriage, and to observe the wide variety of rôles which human beings may be called upon to play. Children from such homes as these, it might be thought, have little need of the vicarious experience which fiction can supply. The only child, on the other hand, the growing child whose brothers and sisters have all left home, the girl who has brothers only, and the boy who has sisters but no brothers, are all to some degree isolated in the home and impoverished in their experience of family living. For these, perhaps, books offer companionship where no other is afforded in the home, and a source of experience which they have no opportunity of gaining at first hand.

Beyond the confines of the family, the nature of the relationships a child forms with other people, children and grown-ups, seems likely to have an important bearing on the matter. On the surface it would seem that the solitary child would be more dependent upon reading than the child who has many friends. Mitchell (1949), however, reporting small but positive correlations between sociability and voluntary reading, comes to the opposite conclusion, that the kind of child who is readily accepted by his fellows is also the kind who reads extensively. We have no direct evidence to offer on this question, but one or two observations made in the course of our enquiry may be thought relevant.

Roughly between the ages of eight and twelve, for girls especially, reading assumes the character of a group activity. Children join together to visit the Library, to exchange books and to discuss them. At this stage, therefore, the reading habit and, for that matter, reading tastes, spread by contagion, and it is possible that the child who in this period does not mix easily with other children may remain untouched. That is not to say, however, that the child who mixes freely will become an unusually avid reader. On the contrary, it is more likely that he will conform quite closely to the practice of his fellows, both in the amount of reading that he does and in the kinds of books he reads. The pressure of prevailing customs and opinions bears strongly upon children at this stage. The cult of Enid Blyton gives an illustration : it has needed no encouragement from adults for her books to become virtually standard reading for children aged from eight to twelve. Children themselves have been the most effective agents in spreading the fashion, and the more closely involved the child is with his age-mates, the more likely he is to follow their example. The solitary child, on the other hand, is more likely to deviate from the common practice, possibly in reading far more or far less than is usual, possibly in reading books which are not generally popular. Children of very high intelligence and those of very low are equally likely, one might suppose, to find themselves excluded from the gang. When considering the reading habits of children such as these, we found them to include some unusually keen readers, and this lends some support to the view that the child who stands apart from his age-mates is likely to read more than the socially acceptable child who adopts the standards of the group.

Linked with this question is that of the relationship between voluntary reading and other leisure activities. That boys read less than girls may well be due, in part, to the fact that many more rival pursuits are available to them. In general, the child who engages in a wide variety of games and hobbies must have less time available for reading, and this is the situation in which the child who has many friends or who is one of a large family must often find himself. There is some evidence,[1] at all events, that children who are given to more

---

[1] Ladd, 1933, p. 10, and p. 43, Table VI.

than the average number of play activities tend to be below average
in educational attainment in general, and in reading ability in particular.
It is likely to be true also of the volume of their leisure reading. It is
not, it must be added, simply a matter of having less time for books ;
children who can express their needs through other play activities will
not have the same motive for reading.

This in turn suggests yet another avenue of enquiry. The relationship between leisure reading and various dimensions of the personality
has not, to our knowledge, been the subject of any systematic study.
Nevertheless, it is not unlikely that the introvert and extravert, for
example, will be found to differ from one another in their reading
tastes and habits in a relatively constant and predictable fashion. It is
possible, too, that each category of maladjustment, neurosis and
delinquency has its own characteristic reading pattern which we shall
some day learn to identify.

Enough has been said, perhaps, to indicate how various are the
influences which go to shape a child's reading behaviour and how
difficult is likely to be the task of isolating any one of the many
factors which plainly are involved. Family size and play activities,
intelligence and social class, these and all others are linked to one
another in a complex inter-play in which each is both cause and effect,
and the personality of the child himself the unique and final outcome.
So it is that to understand a child's reading is hardly less complicated a
task than to understand the child himself.

CHAPTER IX

BILINGUALISM AND LEISURE READING

No enquiry of this sort carried out in Wales can pretend to be complete if it fails to take into account the fact that an appreciable minority of children are to some degree bilingual in English and Welsh. A good deal of research has been done, notably by W. R. Jones (1955), on the reading ability in English of Welsh-speaking children, but no investigation has been made, so far as we have been able to discover, of their leisure-reading habits, although in this connection there are clearly many questions which may have an important bearing on educational policy in a bilingual country. To what extent, for instance, are children who are bilingual in their speech also bilingual in their leisure reading? Do the books a child reads in his first language differ in quantity or quality from those read in his second? Do the answers to these questions depend upon age, intelligence, and facility in either language?

Important though these questions are, and obviously relevant, answers based on a survey limited to a largely anglicised area can at best be tentative, and valuable more as suggesting further lines of enquiry than as offering firm conclusions. While the Language Questionnaire[1] administered to every child revealed that 17 per cent customarily made use of both languages in certain social contexts, a very much smaller number, the seventy-one pupils attending a primary school where Welsh is the medium of instruction, alone had very considerable opportunities for speaking Welsh. Moreover, of the eleven thousand and more library books issued in the year, Welsh books accounted for a mere score, and each of the Welsh readers who borrowed a Welsh book also borrowed English books. Obviously, therefore, the language factor is not of sufficient magnitude to have affected the broad picture of children's reading in this area. A corollary of this, of course, is that, if the numbers are too small to have had an impact on our findings, neither are they large enough to permit of any

---

[1]For a description of the Language Questionnaire employed, see Jones, W. R., et al. (1957. p. 12).

positive conclusions. The evidence now to be offered bearing on this question can claim no degree of statistical reliability ; it affords a glimpse, however, of what promises to be a fruitful field of study, and as such may deserve consideration.

It would appear, much as one might expect, that before the age of ten Welsh-speaking children show less interest in the Library than do monoglots : few of them join, and those who do, borrow very little. This does not mean that these children necessarily read less than others. The Library, it must be borne in mind, caters essentially for English-speaking readers ; although in fact it has a small collection of Welsh books for children, in absolute numbers this is very small and the range of choice available to each Welsh reader is therefore very narrowly restricted. A much richer source of Welsh books is available at school, provided by the Library Service to Schools, and in conse-quence the Welsh child in search of books in Welsh for leisure reading is likely to depend on this rather than upon the Library. Since they tend not to join the Library, it seems reasonable to conclude that, before the age of ten, when reading for pleasure, Welsh-speaking children read mainly books in Welsh.

From the age of ten, on the other hand, so our slender evidence suggests, Welsh-speaking girls tend increasingly to read English books. In the last two years of their primary school lives, they join the Library almost as readily as English-speaking children, and borrow proportionately at least as many books, despite the fact that almost all the books they borrow are in English. The same seems to be true of boys from about the age of nine.

Further research might reveal whether this rather sudden access of interest in English books means a reduction in the number of Welsh books these children read. There is reason to fear that this may be so, if only because of the acute shortage of Welsh books suitable for children. As the publication of Welsh books is a commercial risk, local authorities, as part of their effort to preserve the language, have in recent times given financial support to the production of children's books in Welsh.[1] It is important that the limited funds available for

---

[1]Under the "Five Counties Welsh Books Scheme", local authorities under-take to purchase for schools and libraries a guaranteed number of all children's books published in Welsh. This does not appear to have had the desired effect of stimulating output ; in 1963 only 15 children's books appeared in Welsh, fewer than in previous years. See Caernarvonshire Education Committee : *The County Library, Forty-Sixth Annual Report*, 1963-64, page 8.

this purpose should be used to the best effect, and to this end it would be well to know where the need is greatest. The evidence of the present survey seems to point to the need to make an effort to cater for the ten-year-olds, since it is at this point that Welsh books appear to lose ground to English books, but of course more research is needed to establish whether the trends apparent among bilingual children in the area under review appear in other parts of Wales.

Despite the difficulties, the shortage of Welsh books might conceivably be remedied, but it is by no means certain that this would arrest the drift of Welsh-speaking children towards English books. In a largely anglicised area such as the one in question, from about the age of ten, English tends to assume an increasingly dominant rôle in the lives even of children whose mother tongue is Welsh. Inevitably, from that age, the child makes contact with increasing numbers of people outside the home and school, and thereby is obliged increasingly to use English as the language of social intercourse. This may, and often does, result in the Welsh child's losing the ability to speak his first language, and it is with the express purpose of preventing this that Local Education Authorities have established Welsh-medium primary schools in certain areas throughout Wales. It is a much-debated question whether, in the more anglicised areas, such schools can achieve the purpose for which they were designed. A great deal would seem to depend on there being available to the child a range of leisure activities permitting, or preferably demanding, the use of Welsh. Church services, concerts, films, radio and television programmes, sports organisations and youth clubs must all re-inforce the efforts of the Welsh-language school if the bilingual child is to preserve his first language into later life, and even then success is far from certain. It is to be feared that in this locality at least, to judge from the number of English books they read, Welsh-speaking children, despite being taught in a Welsh school, do not long remain immune against the prevailing anglicising influences. It is not our purpose here to discuss the desirability or otherwise of Welsh-language schools, but to show that research into the leisure reading of bilingual children might have far-reaching implications for educational policy in Wales. Indeed, it might not be too much to say that the extent to which children maintain their interest in Welsh books is a fair measure of the effectiveness of the bilingual policies to which education authorities in Wales are now committed.

To continue the examination of the evidence that is to hand, however, we turn now to the nature of the books these bilingual children choose. It might be expected that, since their education has largely been through the medium of Welsh, and since in consequence they have spent relatively little time on the study of English, the English books they choose for their leisure reading would be rather less demanding than those picked by English-speaking children. Specifically, their choices might be expected to have fewer pages, more illustrations, larger type, and higher scores for Reading Ease than are found in the books chosen by the generality of children of the same age.

In part, these expectations are supported by the evidence. Before the age of ten, bilingual children appear to choose English books which are generally easier than are chosen by monoglots of their own age. The nine-year-old boys, for instance, read books which on average have thirty-five fewer pages, three per cent more pictures, type which is one point larger, and a score for Reading Ease more than four points higher than was found customary at this age. Much the same is true of the nine-year-old girls, and, were this evidence to be relied on, one might conclude that the bilingual nine-year-old reads English books comparable in difficulty to those chosen by the average child of eight. However, at the age of ten and upwards, these differences tend to disappear. This is the case with the number of pages, the amount of illustration and the size of type, at least, but in respect of Reading Ease Welsh-speaking children, even at the age of ten or eleven, appear to choose comparatively simple books.

This suggests a line of enquiry which might well complement, in the field of leisure reading, the work already done by Jones and others on the reading ability of bilingual children. In this respect, Jones (1955) concludes, bilingual children may be as much as ten months in arrears of monoglot English speakers even at the age of ten or eleven, but he is also of the opinion that no such handicap need result when the bilingual's everyday environment offers him sufficient contact with English. In Wales, it is the rural child, rather than the urban child, who is denied this contact, and it is probable that bilingual children resident in towns are not seriously retarded in their English reading in comparison with monoglots. As it happens, the children with whom the present enquiry is concerned are town-dwellers, and this may account for the fact, if indeed it is a fact, that by the age of ten or eleven they no longer appear backward in their leisure reading. At all events, the whole question is one which might with profit be investigated further.

Another question worth considering is whether the kinds of books enjoyed by bilingual children differ significantly in their content from those favoured by monoglots of the same age. Although children living in the same area will to some extent share a common culture, it is also to be expected that with its mother tongue a child will acquire ideals, values and aspirations different in some respects from those associated with another language, and this suggests the possibility that, much as the folk-tales of the Navajo differ from those of the Flatheads, the stories which appeal to Welsh-speaking children will differ from those enjoyed by others.

The evidence, however, in no way bears out this suggestion, but indicates on the contrary an astonishing degree of similarity between the tastes of monoglot and Welsh-speaking children. The books borrowed by Welsh-speaking boys are distributed among the various categories in almost exactly the same proportions as those borrowed by the age-group as a whole. Among the issues to boys, in only two instances are there discrepancies worth noting : at the ages of nine and ten alike, bilingual boys choose fewer works of information than expected, and more tales of Mystery. Similarly, between the girls there are remarkably few differences of note, other than that at the age of ten, Welsh-speaking girls borrow virtually no non-fiction from the Library, and read instead proportionately more fiction—more Family Stories, Careers Stories and Adolescent Novels at the age of ten, more Mystery and Adventure Stories at the age of eleven.

This certainly indicates no profound cultural differences between the two linguistic groups ; on the contrary, it seems to suggest that, despite certain differences in language, schooling, and possibly traditions, boys and girls of a given age have in common dreams, hopes and aspirations which are reflected in a shared interest in books of certain kinds. It must be borne in mind, of course, that all these children, bilinguals and monoglots alike, have sources of reading other than the public library. In particular, it would seem, the Welsh-speaking children resort to the Library almost solely for books in English, and look to other sources for any books they need in Welsh. It is probable, too, that in the primary school stage at least, when reading for information, they tend to turn to books in Welsh, which for them has been the language of instruction, and to read English books predominantly for pleasure. This may prove to be the explanation of the absence of non-fiction among the books they borrow, but to confirm it would require an investigation of the books these children read from other sources than the library, and a comparison of all the books they read in English and in Welsh.

This absence of works of information among books issued to Welsh-speaking readers helps to explain an observation mentioned earlier. It was noted that, although in other respects the books chosen by Welsh boys at the age of nine and ten are very similar to those read by other children, in terms of Reading Ease they are on the whole much simpler. At these ages it will be recalled, the majority of boys borrow a good deal of non-fiction, and in consequence the language of the books they read tends on average to be more difficult. Unlike the majority, however, Welsh-speaking boys borrow no non-fiction, and as a result the books they choose have a higher average score for Reading Ease.

These reflections, necessarily tentative and cautious, so far from constituting final answers, do no more (as was suggested at the outset) than raise questions which seem to call for further study, and which, to produce the answers, would require a survey of leisure-reading habits to be carried out among children living in predominantly Welsh-speaking areas. A great deal more information, obviously, is needed than has hitherto been brought to light. On the evidence available, one is disposed to think that from about the age of ten, Welsh-speaking children turn to English for their leisure reading. Is this in fact the case in areas where the library offers a more adequate selection of Welsh books ? In what classes of books, and for what age-groups, is the shortage of Welsh books most acute ? Is it generally the case that Welsh-speaking children read for information in their mother tongue and read English books for recreation ? If this is so, does it reflect the fact that the supply of works of information in Welsh is less inadequate than the supply of fiction, or is it simply that their command of English is insufficient to enable them to cope with non-fiction in that language ? There is reason to suspect that the shortage of Welsh books is not the whole explanation of the tendency of Welsh speakers to turn to English books as they grow older. Is this an inevitable result of their growing contact, after the early years of childhood, with the English-speaking community ? Is there any difference, that is to say, in this respect between children living in a rural, hence virtually monoglot, Welsh area and those living in an urban area ? Nothing has come to light which shows that Welsh-speaking children differ in their reading tastes from English-speaking children of the same age. Is it in fact the case that linguistic differences have no effect ? When bilingual children have equal access to books in either language, are those they read in Welsh similar in level of difficulty, in their themes and in their treatment, to those they read in English ?

The main difficulty in the way of finding answers to these questions is likely to arise as a result of the disparity between the numbers of Welsh and English books available. A child with only a moderate appetite for reading could well exhaust the score or so of Welsh books for children produced each year, and, since most of these are intended for the very young, the child of ten or eleven who is to any degree an avid reader may have little choice but to read English publications. In consequence, it may prove difficult to assess the true nature and extent of children's interest in Welsh books, but the effort would appear well worth making, since it might provide the key to a number of important problems in the field of bilingual education, and have a practical application to the task of preserving the Welsh language. In the light of such an enquiry it might be possible not only to decide, as was suggested earlier, on what types of books it were best to concentrate the slender resources available for encouraging Welsh publications, but also to observe with some minuteness the process by which the Welsh-speaking child is weaned to English, and, if it be proved desirable to arrest this process, to find the most effective means of doing so.

CHAPTER X

WHY CHILDREN READ

THE purposes for which people read may be considered as falling into three broad classes. Firstly, they read for information : they consult dictionaries, time-tables and directories in order to solve an immediate practical problem—to check a spelling, to catch a train, or to find an address. Secondly, they read for education, to effect changes within themselves, to develop abilities and skills. Still present, though more remote, is the practical and conscious purpose—to repair a car, to pass an examination, or to train for an occupation. Finally, they read for recreation, with no other conscious purpose than that of gaining pleasure. In practice, of course, it is rarely possible to separate the three. Not infrequently, the reader derives pleasure from the books he reads ostensibly for information ; he may also gain some educational benefit—an increased command of words, for instance—from those he reads expressly for enjoyment. In any case, he may not always be aware of, or able to express, all the motives which impel him to read a given book.

This is especially true of the books he reads allegedly for pleasure. More often than not, this is the only purpose of which children are aware when choosing their library books. To be sure, they sometimes choose a book for information or instruction, and to the extent that it serves their purpose, they find it enjoyable to read. In this case, their pleasure is the outcome of their having achieved their purpose ; it is a by-product, so to speak, of other satisfactions. Even when they read for recreation, however, the pleasure they experience is again incidental, a sign that other purposes have been served. This means, in effect, that reading affords pleasure either when it serves some quite explicit purpose, or when it satisfies in some way certain deeper and less conscious needs, and, in fact, the more intense the pleasure, the less likely is the reader to be able to explain its cause.

At the more conscious level, children read to make their universe intelligible. They look for pattern, order and consistency in the world, because without them there can be no sense of security. The child's love of rhythm, repetition and routine springs from this need for order and stability, and the virtue of a book lies partly in the fact that it imposes logic and system upon brute reality. It is easy enough to see how works of information serve this purpose. As a child progresses from Morey's *Old MacDonald's Farm*, which he reads at the age of five or six, to *Out with Romany by moor and dale* by G. B. Evens at the age of nine or ten, and to Crommelin's *Story of the stars*, which may attract him at the age of eleven or twelve, we can readily understand that his reading is a means of enlarging his understanding of the world in which he lives. His fiction, too, contributes to this purpose. We have seen how his early stories help him to understand the complexities of domestic life, while later ones introduce him to life at school or to the world of work. Obviously, the younger the child, the simpler the picture of the world must be. For the very young, it is necessary that the book portray the world as black and white, good and evil, obvious cause and inevitable effect ; but even in the more complex works read by older children, there is a plan and pattern not immediately apparent in the real world, and this explains how they contribute to a child's sense of security in the puzzling and mysterious world.

The child reads, then, to understand the significance of his experience, to feel at home in an ordered and purposive universe. But more than that, he reads to meet the future, to rehearse the problems he will face tomorrow. Much depends, of course, on the degree of anxiety or eagerness with which the child looks forward to the future. It is of the essence of all fiction that it sets reality at a safe distance, and the younger, the less experienced and the less secure the child, the greater must that distance be. The more apprehensive the child, that is to say, the less realistic will be the image he is prepared to face. In the natural order of events, however, anxiety gives way to eagerness and finally to matter-of-fact acceptance. Fantasy, romance and realism reflect in turn each of these attitudes and help the child to make the transition. More obviously, perhaps, in sharing vicariously in the experiences of characters more mature than himself, a child reveals that part of his purpose in reading is to anticipate the future and to fit himself for the task of growing up.

An essential part of growing up is the process of discovering one's own identity. Two things are here involved : on the one hand, the plumbing of one's inner impulses and resources ; on the other, the reviewing of the rôles it is possible to play. By projecting himself into various fictional situations, the reader makes explicit to himself his own capacity for fear, courage, pity, cruelty, love and hate, and, by assuming in turn the identity of many different characters, finally fashions for himself his own ' self-image '. This prescribes for him the upper limit beyond which it would be unrealistic to aspire, and the lower limit below which he cannot fall without loss of self-respect.

Even in their fiction, then, children pursue information and skills which will enable them to fill more adequately the various rôles they elect or believe themselves obliged to play. The ability to read itself is one such skill. It carries great prestige, especially for the very young, and most children are prepared to do some private reading simply in order to acquire it. We may guess, too, that the principal pleasure some older children of limited intelligence derive from borrowing books is that it vindicates their claim to be good readers. Others, notably perhaps among the boys, appear to read chiefly because they believe it will help them in their work at school. It is significant that many children take to attending the library shortly before secondary selection, and fall away when the effort proves not to have produced the desired result. However, it is much more common for a child to read for purposes other than the purely scholastic, in the service, for example, of some hobby or some sport.

All these are among the more obvious and explicit of the purposes for which children read. Somewhat less articulate are the emotional needs they seek to satisfy through reading. By identifying himself with a fictional character and participating in imagination in the character's activities, the reader can achieve a satisfying, though vicarious, experience of parental love, of friendship, of success, of freedom from restraint, needs which are common to all children as to other human beings. They are not normally repressed ; on the contrary, they can be acknowledged and indulged quite openly, and books designed for children need make no disguise of the fact that their appeal is to desires of this kind. The reader himself, too, though he may not consciously have chosen the book to meet these needs, may in retrospect be quite aware of the real reasons for his pleasure in it.

Children, however, even as do adults, read at different levels, often simultaneously. If, at one level, the reader is engaged in the pursuit of quite conscious ends, and at another seeks to satisfy certain less articulate, emotional needs, at a still deeper level the imagination is ceaselessly scanning the book for what will give expression to other repressed

and unacknowledged impulses. A process which Lesser[1] calls 'Analogizing' is at work. The reader unconsciously seizes upon some parallel
between the fictional situation and his own, or some resemblance
between himself and one of the characters, and thereafter the whole
work begins to function as an allegory wherein, symbolically, problems
he finds insuperable in reality are solved, unexpressed anxieties are
allayed and frustrated desires are gratified.

Even when a child is reading a severely factual work, there is sometimes reason to suspect that his real interest is not in the book's apparent,
but in its latent, content, and that the satisfactions it affords him are
essentially subliminal. The following are some of the titles borrowed
by one boy aged nine : *The how and why aeroplane book* ; *Insect life* ;
The boy's book of locomotives ; *Our merchant navy* ; others dealt with
archaeology, handicrafts and wild life. This wide-ranging curiosity
about the physical and natural world is by no means unusual in boys
of this age, and would ordinarily be regarded as part of the child's
attempt, once he has established a firm base of security in the home
and in the world immediately around, to push his investigations into
the world beyond. The only work of fiction borrowed by this boy,
however, is a story entitled *Boo, the boy who didn't like the dark*, a
simple picture-book fairly popular with five- and six-year olds but
rarely read by older children. This must give us pause. Does not this
one title put all the others in a different light ? Does this child's
reading spring from a bold desire to explore the whole wide world, or
is it part of his effort to reduce all the things he fears to a series of
harmless pictures in a book ? It is evident, at all events, that one would
need to look far below the surface to find the true explanation of his
choices.

This is even more true of the fiction a child reads. Admittedly,
before a child chooses a particular story, its manifest content must
make some appeal to his waking mind, but it makes its most powerful
impact on the reader when, beneath this surface interest, unconscious
needs and longings are afforded satisfaction. The enjoyment of fiction
entails a surrender to the illusion it seeks to create, a certain relaxation
of the critical faculties, a partial withdrawal from reality and a temporary dispensation from the laws and prohibitions that apply in it. We
more readily succumb to its suggestion when our minds are not coast-

---

[1]Lesser (1960), p. 10.

antly alert to grapple with difficulties of language and other complexities, and this perhaps explains why children prefer the language and
content of their stories to be simple, though they are prepared to
accept a fair degree of difficulty in their works of information. A work
of fiction, to make its full hallucinatory effect, needs to be read almost
automatically ; laborious, effortful reading, does, quite literally, break
the spell and disrupts the process of analogizing which is the source of
the powerful emotional satisfactions the reading of stories commonly
permits.

All this is to imply, in effect, that a child's reading, however in-
consequential and purposeless it may seem, plays a vital part in his
effort to come to terms with the external world and his own nature,
and the satisfactions he pursues in reading are not essentially different
from those he seeks in life itself. At whatever level he reads, however,
and for whatever motive, the experiences which books provide and
the rewards they offer can be no more than substitutes for those which
reality affords, and the question that arises is why they should be
desirable or necessary.

One answer is, of course, that they are purchased with less effort and
at less risk than those of real life. In the world of fiction, the reader
triumphs without exertion, gains love and friendship without exposing
himself to rebuff, and earns admiration without putting himself to any
test. Reading of this kind is a form of self-indulgence, a holiday from
effort. It is rather like eating chocolate after a good meal : it does not
meet a hungry need, but echoes and prolongs the pleasurable sensation
of fulfilment. There is no urgency in reading of this kind ; its function
is not to meet a need which otherwise would be unsated, but to
renew for the reader, in a more intense and pure form perhaps, the
satisfactions he already knows. In short, it is not the product of
frustration but a form of relaxation.

Secondly, of course, the range of experiences and the variety of
satisfactions reading offers are much wider than are available to any
one person in reality. No-one is free, in real life, to gratify his every
wish ; all must submit at times, whether to practical necessity, to
natural laws or to the pressures of society. And however readily, for
the most part, we renounce the inaccessible, inevitably there are times
when our confinement becomes irksome, when our present way of
life seems to have yielded all it has to offer and we yearn for new
worlds to conquer. The reader, in imagination, can transcend all

barriers, flout all prohibitions, experience the forbidden. It is sometimes possible to detect the impatience of restriction, the longing to
escape, the thirst for freedom to which a child seeks to give expression
in his reading. He turns to books because they promise him emancipation.

They also offer compensation, redress the defeats and deprivations
he has known in real life. In much of children's reading, wish-fulfilment plays a part : the friendless child finds friends in books, the
insecure child a happy family. But books hold out more than simple
consolation ; they allow the reader to forget failure and humiliation
and to salve his self-esteem by taking to himself the attributes and
triumphs of a character in fiction. The hall-mark of such reading is
usually its extravagant unreality, the gross incongruity between the
reader and the character with whom he identifies. The child who
cannot make friends may imagine herself to be a school-girl film-star,
the insecure child an outlaw chief. When a child reads for relaxation or
emancipation, there is still some correspondence between the satisfactions he requires from books and those he aspires to in actuality.
When he reads for compensation, on the other hand, he seeks rewards
far richer than any he expects from life itself.

Finally, books provide the reader with a refuge from his every-day
existence. Over-taxed by the demands of daily living or rebuffed in
his efforts to come to terms with other people, he can turn to books and
find, not a solution to his problems, but escape from them. In reading
he recovers the uncomplicated and indulgent world he knew in
infancy, and finds again the magic key to security and happiness. It
gives him respite from the task of growing up, and allows him to
retreat once more to childhood. The books he chooses for this purpose
will often be markedly less difficult, in language, themes and treatment,
than is appropriate to his age or ability, but the key-note of such reading
is not its immaturity, but its studious avoidance of all contact with
actuality. In many cases, human beings have no place in the books he
chooses ; in others human beings are endowed with magical or superhuman attributes, the worlds they inhabit are fantastic or, failing that,
exotic and remote, and their activities and way of life quite unrelated
to the reader's waking world. Regressive reading of this kind may
have the air of a neurotic refusal to face reality, but it must be remembered that reading is only part of an individual's response to
circumstances. A temporary withdrawal into fantasy may well be a

necessary preparation for a renewed and more effective assault upon his problems. At the same time, if a child's reading is habitually of this kind, it argues some anxiety, some personal inadequacy on his part, arising from some chronic difficulty in meeting life's demands.

It sometimes happens that all or most of a child's recreative reading is directed towards one or other of the forms of wish-fulfilment which we have termed relaxation, emancipation, compensation and regression. However, this calls for a certain capacity for self-surrender, a readiness to be 'carried away' by reading, of which some children seem incapable. Sometimes a child lacks that automatic fluency in reading which makes possible the absorption and self-forgetfulness which books appealing to the imagination seek to induce. In other cases it may mean that the child has too precarious a grip on reality to take the risk of surrendering to illusion. This timidity is characteristic of the very young, for whom it is not always easy to separate fact from fancy, and whose perplexity on this score may lead to anxiety and distress. Many a parent, seeking to console a child to whom the reading of a story has brought fear or grief, has found that to try to explain that the story is after all not real, so far from bringing comfort, serves to increase his perturbation. It is necessary to the child's sense of security that he should be able to distinguish clearly between what is real and what is not, and younger readers, for whom this distinction is not easy, tend to prefer stories which make no attempt to disguise their fictitious nature. The Puppet and the Fairy Story appeal to such children precisely because there is no confusing the world they describe with the real world.

Among older children, too, there are some who seem reluctant to be lulled into an acceptance of illusion and who are chary of losing sight of reality. It manifests itself in a strong inclination to read factual works and a tendency to avoid all forms of fiction other than the Puppet and the Fairy Story. The boy of nine whose reading was described above is a fairly typical example of a kind of reader more commonly to be found among children of a very low intelligence.[1] It will be recalled

---

[1]Lesser (1960, p. 49, et seq.), arguing that a certain reduction of control is necessary to the enjoyment of fiction, suggests that a chronic inability to 'let go' implies a weak ego organisation, "a fear that if the ego relaxed even a trifle it could not maintain order in its own house". Weak ego organisation is certainly to be expected in the very young, and possibly, though I am not aware of any evidence on the point, in those of low intelligence.

that such children combine an unusual fondness for purely factual works with what appears at first sight an incompatible taste for ostentatiously unrealistic stories. The explanation appears to be that they distrust any book which blurs the distinction between the real and the imaginary ; they share with the very young a literal-mindedness which renders them incapable of that voluntary suspension of disbelief, that unreserved surrender to its spell, which the more realistic, 'human' fiction calls for.

The pattern of his reading, therefore, sometimes reveals that a child finds it difficult to give free rein to his imagination. Most children, however, appear to have no such inhibition and welcome the opportunity which fiction affords of unrestrained indulgence in wishful thinking. In some children it takes the form of a constant search for relaxation. Such readers conspicuously avoid any book which strains their understanding or calls for a powerful emotional response. Typically, the books they choose deal, in fairly realistic terms, with children of their own age, at school or on holiday by the sea or in the country, involved in circumstances and activities which might feasibly be within their own experience. They do not, that is to say, significantly enlarge the child's horizons or plumb new depths of thought and feeling ; instead, they shed a golden light upon the world with which he is familiar and double his contentment with his lot. Clearly, these readers are not driven by any devouring curiosity, any strong sense of deprivation or any profound emotional stress. For the most part, they appear to be happy, well-adjusted children, of average intelligence or more, and under no obvious handicap in their efforts to meet the demands of day-to-day existence. Among them, for example, are a number of highly intelligent grammar school girls, whose reading, it will be recalled, is so undemanding and light-hearted as to be almost self-indulgence.

To illustrate this type of reading, an example may be taken from among the boys. David, the only child of middle-class parents, had an Intelligence score of 120, and in his final year at the primary school, during which he qualified for admission to the grammar school, was said to work successfully, to be happy and well-behaved. He was a regular though not a voracious reader of library books, and between his eleventh and twelfth birthdays borrowed twenty-four, among them four works on handicrafts, including puppetry, for children. His fiction comprised one work of fantasy—Barbara Euphan Todd's

Worzel Gummidge, the story of a scare-crow which comes to life—three Mystery Stories, and sixteen Gang Stories, all of them *William* stories by Richmal Crompton. There seems little in David's reading to challenge his understanding, stretch his imagination or deeply stir his feelings. In terms of Reading Ease, those of Richmal Crompton, with scores between 65 and 70, are the most difficult of the books he reads ; he never tries to imagine himself in some completely strange environment or to assume a personality quite different from his own. On the contrary, much of his pleasure in this fictional experience springs from his recognition of its familiarity. His choices are restricted to a very narrow field and, significantly, rather than sampling a new author or an unaccustomed theme, he returns repeatedly to books read previously. One of his Mystery titles re-appears some months later, as does a book on handicrafts, while *William's Happy Days*, which gives the key-note to almost all his reading, occurs three times in the year.

It is illuminating to compare David's reading with that of Michael, again an only child with a very similar home back-ground, apparently happy and reasonably successful at school, but almost exactly a year younger than David, and with an Intelligence score of only 94. By no means an inveterate reader, he borrowed only nineteen books in the year, eleven of them non-fiction. The latter included one book on local geography and two others on the geography of the world ; two books on castles, and an abridged version of Froissart's chronicles ; two on birds and another on wild animals, Wallace's *Boy's Book of Science and Invention*, and a collection of Arthurian legends. His fiction consisted, apart from one juvenile Mystery Story by Enid Blyton, entirely of Adventure Stories of the kind in which the adolescent hero faces dangers by the side of grown men in remote corners of the world. What is immediately noticeable is how much more ambitious, despite his relative youth and low intelligence, Michael's reading is than that of David. His imagination is obviously outward-looking and yet, such is the balance and variety in his choice of books, there is no sense of deep frustration or of an obsessional desire for escape. The impression given is of a child who copes confidently and happily with his present circumstances, who has a healthy eagerness to face the future, and whose reading is, unconsciously if not by design, part of his preparation for growing up and going out into the world. For Michael, as perhaps for the majority of children, reading is primarily a means to emancipation ; in some, however, the sense of frustration and the yearning for escape to which their reading gives expression is more obviously urgent and obsessive.

Not every reader shows the same confidence and freedom from anxiety as do both Michael and David in their different ways. For the boy of nine already mentioned, reading is a form of whistling in the dark ; the bold front it helps him to put on fails to disguise the fears that lurk beneath. Others, too, who are for some reason unable to participate effectively in the activities and experiences common to their fellows, or who doubt their own ability to meet the demands made on them, may read to bolster up their self-esteem, to over-compensate their sense of inadequacy. The air of bravado, of extravagant boasting that pervades their reading, itself betrays their inner doubts and their need for reassurance. Something of this was evident in the attitude of the boys of very limited intelligence referred to in a previous chapter, but an example may serve to illustrate what is characteristic of this approach to books.

Janice, the middle child of three in a manual worker's family, had an Intelligence score of 114, and, having done quite well in her first year at the secondary modern school, was transferred at the age of 13 years 5 months to the first form of the grammar school. She did not join the library until two months after her admission, and in the remaining ten months of the year took out thirty-three books—three works of non-fiction on horsemanship, six Pony Stories, one jungle and sixteen western Adventure Stories, and seven Animal Stories. All except three of the stories she chose are set in the jungle or the far west ; only rarely is the central character a girl and in many cases no female characters at all appear ; a wild animal, usually a horse, but sometimes a tiger, elephant or lion, plays a prominent part in nearly every book. In all these respects, her tastes differ markedly from those of most girls of her age and even more from those of the majority in her form. She has no interest in the School Story, the Family Story, the Careers story or the Adolescent Novel ; she shares to some extent their fondness for the Pony Story, but even so prefers stories charged with symbolism, such as *The Silver Quest* by Elizabeth Bleecker Meigs, to the straight-forward tales of hunting and riding of the Pullein-Thompsons. Some of her titles are revealing : *Striped Majesty, Wild Horse, Dark Fury, Capture of the Golden Stallion, The Golden Stallion's Victory*. A dominant theme in these and many others of her stories is perhaps most clearly exemplified in René Guillot's *Sama*, the story of a young elephant, son of the leader of the herd and his queen, who, captured and sent to a circus, stubbornly refuses to be tamed, and finally escapes back to the jungle.

The parallel between this and the situation of a girl removed from one school and placed among younger children in another is not difficult to find, nor is it hard to see that in her reading Janice repeatedly asserts her proud independence, her haughty rejection of the herd, her indomitable refusal to conform. But, one may think, she protests too much ; the very extravagance of the terms in which she declares her indifference to her peers betrays her longing for friendship and acceptance. It is this extravagance, this gross disparity between the reader's actual situation and the situation as his books allow him to imagine it, that marks the child who reads for compensation.

The angry self-assertiveness that sounds throughout Janice's reading is quite absent from Patricia's. Two years younger than Janice, and in her last year at the primary school, she borrowed in all twenty-six books from the library. The one work of information among them— on book-production—she did not enjoy ; she liked *New Tales of Robin Hood* but not *The Settlers of Carriacou*, the other of the two Adventure Stories she took out ; she read no Family Story, no Mystery, no Gang or Pony Stories, and only one of the School Stories so popular among her age-mates. Her choices include five Puppet Stories, of which *Little Pig Barnaby and Other Stories* is a fairly typical example ; five modern Fairy Stories, among them Barrie's *Peter Pan and Wendy* ; eight traditional fairy tales such as *The Three Princesses of Whiteland* ; *The Book of the Cat Jeremiah* and two similar Animal Stories ; finally, Arthur Mee's *Children's Life of Jesus*.

Patricia seems to have no difficulty in reading : she prefers collections of short stories, it is true, but all her books are of substantial length and some of them are fairly difficult. That is not what gives her reading its air of childishness, but her complete refusal to make the slightest overture to other children or to older people, or in any way to acknowledge the real world around. Her absorption is that of a child smiling over her toys and dolls, all else forgotten. This is not the reading of a confident child, eager for experience and for self-fulfilment, but of one all too conscious of her own inadequacies, all too vulnerable to failure and rejection, seeking only refuge from reality and from herself in the indulgent world of fantasy. Patricia's choices have much in common with those of the girls of very limited intelligence referred to in an earlier chapter, and it comes as no surprise that her Intelligence score is only 88 ; perhaps even more revealing is the fact that she is the younger of the two children of a widowed mother, her father having died when she was nine.

Each of the four readers here described exhibits a distinctive attitude to reading, an attitude which reflects, and is determined by, the degree to which his or her experience of reality has proved happy and fulfilling. The child who has confidence in himself and is basically contented with his situation, will tend to read for relaxation ; another, equally self-confident but more rebellious, for emancipation ; one, disappointed in his hopes, retrieves his self-esteem and silences his inner doubts by finding compensation in his reading ; another, anxious and insecure in an inhospitable world, reads for regression. It is not surprising, therefore, that intelligent middle-class children should, by and large, read for relaxation, intelligent working-class children for emancipation, dull middle-class children for compensation, and dull working-class children for regression. Though this may be acceptable as a generalisation, it must be stressed once more that none of these attitudes is confined to children of a certain level of ability or of any one social class ; the dull child may be as happy as the bright, and the child from a prosperous home may be more seriously deprived than the child in the most unpromising surroundings. We cannot, therefore, predict that a child with a given social background and level of ability will read in a certain way, but we can say that a child's characteristic approach to reading is explicable as part of his total response to his environment and situation.

It must be said, however, that the pattern of reading is seldom as straightforward as in the four examples given. It is not usual for an individual's reading to be exclusively of one kind or another, although, as has been said, boys tend to restrict their choices to a narrower range than girls. Only rarely is it possible to say of a child that his reading affords clear evidence of chronic anxiety, chronic frustration, or chronic inadequacy. While, in some cases, an intense obsession with a certain theme may point to this, for the most part each separate act of choice a child will make is the outcome of a unique combination of factors : the mood of the moment, the passing interest, the immediate problem and a host of other imponderables may go to determine which book will be picked at any time, and the more permanent dispositions and preoccupations of the reader are to be divined only from certain themes and motifs which recur insistently in his reading over a long period.

Another qualification must be made. Reading is, in any case, only part of a child's response to his environment, and to assess it in isolation from his total behaviour may lead to a false view of the purpose it fulfils in the child's life. For some, quite obviously, it plays a major part in their effort to accommodate themselves to life's demands ; for others, some other activity performs this rôle, and reading itself serves only trivial functions. Not inconceivably, therefore, one might find at one extreme a child who displays a justifiable confidence in real life but whose reading, regarded separately, might seem to reveal acute anxiety, and at the other extreme a child whose reading betrays no sign of the deep disturbances that are obvious in the rest of his behaviour. Two things are implied in this. In the first place, it would be wrong to regard a child's reading as the sole, or even as the most important, symptom of his emotional state and outlook, helpful though it might be in reaching an assessment. And secondly, a child's reading must ultimately be judged in the context of the child's own life and by its effects upon his mode of dealing with his problems. From a standpoint other than the strictly academic, what is important is not what a child reads but how he lives, and when it falls to us to prescribe books for children, we should be guided not so much by our assessment of a book's literary worth as by our judgement of its relevance to the reader's situation and his needs.

CHAPTER XIII

GUIDING CHILDREN'S READING

W E embarked on this enquiry from a profound belief in the importance of reading in children's lives, and in its potential value as a means to their intellectual, moral and emotional maturity. At the same time, it seemed chasteningly evident that the vast amount of time spent in reading instruction and in the encouragement of reading habits among children results all too often in their forsaking reading as they enter adolescence, or in their becoming, as adults, voracious readers of nothing but the trivial. It was our hope that a clearer understanding of the processes by which reading tastes and habits mature might enable us to suggest policies which would have a more successful outcome. It remains now to be seen whether any conclusions of value to the parent, the teacher and the librarian can be drawn from our investigation.

A wide discrepancy exists between what teachers, and others concerned with fostering the reading habit, believe to be the purposes to which reading ought properly to be directed, and the functions which, in practice, it performs in children's lives. We see, all too clearly perhaps, the value of reading for some obviously practical or vocational end—for information or education, but find it difficult to concede that reading for mere recreation may have any merit other than the pleasure it affords and the added fluency it brings. The evidence adduced in previous chapters shows this to be too narrow and superficial a conception, and draws particular attention to the important part such reading plays in children's emotional development.

The trouble has been that for social reasons reading has come to be valued for itself. Modern society demands of its citizens the ability to read, and sets itself to foster reading skills and reading habits. This, since the educational reforms of the last century, has been seen as the basic task of our primary schools, and in it they have been abetted by our public libraries, for the society which in the last century saw the need for universal literacy also saw the need to make books easily available. Teachers and librarians, therefore, in promoting reading skills and in encouraging the reading habit, have been performing a necessary social task, but in the process have sometimes adopted too restricted a view of their functions and have neglected the value of reading as a means to better living on the part of individuals and of society. This is less true perhaps of teachers than of librarians, who are sometimes heard to disclaim any responsibility for improving cultural standards, and to proclaim it as their task simply to supply the public with what it demands, with the result that the public library is in some danger of becoming just another of the agencies of mass entertainment not essentially different from the commercial cinema. Against this it needs to be asserted that reading should be much more than a pastime, that reading for reading's sake is not enough, since to read for pleasure only, and with no other aim, is to be a slave to reading as some are slaves to eating, and that to be fully master of the reading habit is to read with conscious purpose to enhance the quality of our daily lives.

Children, at all events, expect more of their reading than mere entertainment. They read, as this enquiry has made evident, to gain increased proficiency in reading ; they read, too, for information and instruction in a fairly narrow, utilitarian sense, but, if their reading serves no other purpose, these aims are not sufficient in themselves to sustain an abiding interest in books. Consider the many children who were seen to forsake the Library once they failed to gain admission to the grammar school. Presumably these children derived pleasure from their reading, but clearly they expected in addition that it would be of value to them in their school careers. When this proved vain, the pleasure books had given them was not enough to prevent their leaving the Library. At the same time, reading for mere instruction is no more likely to lead to a continuing interest in books ; it seems evident that children who choose only works of information rarely develop a strong appetite for reading. It is reasonable, therefore, to conclude that it is a mistake on the part of teachers and librarians, when dealing with children of primary school age, to concentrate too narrowly upon the immediate, practical benefits of reading—on reading for information and for education in the more obvious sense ; it is equally a mistake to regard reading simply as a form of entertainment ; to do either is likely ultimately to be self-defeating, since on neither can be founded an enduring and worthwhile interest in books.

Why is it, then, that some children do acquire a strong and wholesome interest in reading ? What do they find in books that makes reading of abiding value to them ? Our whole enquiry has turned upon this question, but the following two cases may help us to summarise our answer. Both are boys whom we first meet when they enter Standard V in their primary school. Both are of only moderate ability, and at the beginning of next year they will both find themselves in the secondary modern school. Both are members of the Public Library.

The first begins the year by borrowing Enid Blyton's *Mystery of the Hidden House*. Three months later, he is reading Enid Blyton's *Lucky Story Book* ; three months later still, it is Blyton's *Sunny Story Book*, and at the end of the year he is back where he began, with Enid Blyton's *Mystery of the Hidden House*. In all he borrowed 74 books in the year, 38 of them by Blyton. In the following year, he borrowed none at all. It need not be doubted that he enjoyed his reading, but it got him nowhere, and so he gave it up. And this, perhaps, is not entirely to be regretted ; others, less wise or less fortunate, fail to break the habit, but obsessively continue looking for they know not what, reading ever more futilely until at last they become incurably addicted to reading-matter of the most ephemeral kind.

Look, by way of contrast, at the second boy. He begins the year in much the same way, with Enid Blyton's *Mystery of Tally-ho Cottage*. In the following five weeks, he runs through ten books by Enid Blyton in a row, and then moves on to other tales of mystery and adventure by John Kennett, F. W. Dixon, Eric Leyland and others, reading altogether 43 books in the year, and finishing with *Biggles Takes the Case*, an adventure story with an adult hero, by W. E. Johns. The following year he rejoined the Library and took out a further 27 books. Whereas the first boy's reading was static or regressive, finally to be rejected as being of no value, this second boy had stumbled by some chance upon the secret of progressive reading ; his reading grew with him and played a part in the process of his growth. That, it is suggested, is why he felt reading to be important to him, and that is why his interest in books survived.

The healthy reader, then, is one whose reading is progressive, whose reading tastes change constantly to match his growing capacity to grasp ideas, his growing interest in other people, his growing urge to understand himself, his own ambitions, powers and responsibilities. Because he finds the books that are responsive to his needs, his reading is of value and he becomes a constant reader. Others, however, fail to accommodate their reading to the pace of their intellectual, emotional and imaginative development, and in consequence their reading makes no contribution to the shaping of their lives. Some recognise it then as trivial, and look elsewhere for what they need ; others accept it as a pastime, to be abandoned when a more diverting pastime offers ; still others read themselves into a rut, the endlessly repetitive, un-progressive, unproductive reading of the addict.

We look to books, that is to say, in an effort to find satisfaction for certain needs within ourselves, but, it is well we should remember, reading can be both nourishment and palliative. It nourishes when it not only satisfies our needs but strengthens us for further effort ; it is a palliative when it assuages our needs but leaves us no fitter than before to meet the tasks of living. The chief needs which children seek, in common with all other human beings, are for security, for status and for self-realisation. By security is meant freedom from anxiety, some understanding of, and control over, the circumstances in which one lives. Status implies the good opinion of other human beings, an assured and valued part to play among them, the self-respect that comes from an awareness of one's own significance and purpose. Self-realisation entails the recognition of oneself as similar to, but distinguished from, all other human beings, some sense of being a unique, autonomous and unfettered individual, free to grow and to develop in accordance to what one feels to be the laws of one's own nature.

Childhood, however, is an age of insecurity, of subjection and of conformity. For a brief while, the child may find complete fulfilment within the narrow confines of the home, but inexorably his needs outgrow the home's capacity to satisfy them, and at the same time he is made aware of, and is forced to adapt himself to, a world far larger than that of his immediate knowledge, more complex, more myster-ious, less stable, less predictable, less subject to his personal control. He finds that the small world of his personal experience is but a poor and partial reflection of the world outside ; the world into which he is born, so to speak, is no true image of the world into which he must grow. The range of experience available to him in the home comes to appear too limited ; it neither challenges his curiosity nor offers scope for the exercise of his growing powers. At the same time he comes to realise that he is ill-equipped for living in a wider society ; the know-ledge and the skills it calls for cannot be acquired in the home, the sentiments and values learnt at home are inappropriate abroad, his attitudes and relationships to others in the family have no place in his dealings with those he meets outside. On the one hand, then, the real world, the world of his direct experience, is inadequate to his needs, nor, on the other, can it fit him for the wider world. Poised, as it were, on the edge of this wider, unknown life, the child turns to books, for reading, like play, is a sort of rehearsal for living ; in it he acquires the knowledge, the skills, the self-control and self-understanding needed for his growth. In this way, his reading serves his need for information, for education and for self-realisation, and to the extent that it meets these vital needs it also gives him pleasure. This pleasure, for the healthy reader, is an incidental gain, a by-product of the satisfaction of some deeper need, whereas to read for the sole purpose of enjoyment is a form of self-indulgence which renders the reader increasingly incapable of truly profiting from books, and does nothing to make him more effective in his daily life.

What, in effect, is here implied is that reading, as well as being a source of pleasure, cannot fail to have an effect, for good or ill, upon our daily lives, and that it is by these effects, rather than by the enjoyment it affords, that children's reading should be judged. Good reading is reading which not only gives the reader pleasure, but enables him to grow.

It is capable of doing so precisely because the world conjured up by books differs from the real world in ways which make it more apt to meet the needs of childhood. In the first place, the picture of the universe which books present may be truer and more comprehensive than the child can gather from his limited experience ; and secondly, in that world he can explore, experiment, and try his powers, without fear of the disasters that might attend such efforts in the real world. At the same time, of course, the reading habit has its dangers. The image of the world which books present is not always true, and when that is so the responses learnt from books may lead to failure in reality. This is obviously the case with books read for purposes of information or of education : the railway guide was faulty, and we therefore miss our train ; the course-book was misleading, so the French we write is bad. It is no less true of books which children read for recreation : when the stories a child chooses falsify reality, distort the picture of human relations, or offer him a false scale of values, if they have any influence at all upon his life, it can only be for ill.

There is another danger, which arises from the fact that the world of books is a safe world, in which the reader may live vicariously the life he chooses, without effort and without risk. The passive reader, he who reads, not with conscious purpose, but for unconscious motives which he neither understands nor controls, comes to prefer illusion to reality ; his reading then becomes an addiction, an end in itself, and its effect is not to equip him better to lead his real life but to enable him to evade the effort of meeting its demands. One can sympathise with Flaubert's Emma Bovary and Cervantes's Don Quixote, misguided though they may have been in their attempts to lead in real life the romantic existences they had read about in books. At least it can be said of them that in their lives they tried to pursue the ideals, however false, they had acquired through their reading. One can sympathise too with the woman who, in our own day, identifies herself in her imagination with the heroines of the novelettes she reads, and thereby escapes briefly from the weariness and drabness of her daily life. For children, however, reading can do so much more that it is surely a waste of opportunity not to do everything that can be done to ensure that it is directed to better ends.

This implies, however, a measure of control over children's leisure-reading to which some may take exception on the ground that it encroaches upon one of the few remaining areas in which children are free to pursue their own devices. This objection is not to be answered lightly, since it asserts what we take to be a fundamental principle in education, the sanctity of the individual and his right to the free expression of his personality. At the same time, in education, this respect for the child as an individual does not imply a policy of laisser-faire : the teacher's role is not passive or neutral ; on the contrary, he is positively committed to take what steps he may to ensure the full flowering of his charge's personality. In the field of reading, specifically, he exerts his influence in the class-room to instil habits of discrimination which he hopes will be carried over into private reading, and it is no fault of his if the effect of what is read at school is out-weighed by the sheer bulk of what is read outside. Even the average reader, it must be remembered, between five and thirteen years of age, seems to borrow from the Public Library about twenty books a year, a much larger number than he reads in class.

No violation of basic principles, therefore, is involved in extending educational guidance to cover children's private reading. To say this, however, is not enough ; some much more positive argument must be adduced to warrant interference in a child's right to follow his own inclinations. It is justifiable only to the extent that it results in his becoming, in reading as in all other matters, an autonomous, self-directing individual, one who consciously controls his own actions and decisions, and is slave neither to influences from without nor to unconscious impulses from within. Individual freedom, as an educational ideal, postulates self-knowledge and self-control ; it is meaningful only to the person who has a clear understanding of his own nature, his inner needs and resources, interests and motives. It is precisely because a child's recreational reading can, and indeed often does, play so vital a part in this process of self-discovery that we believe it should not be entirely haphazard.

We can legitimately seek to influence children's reading, therefore, provided that our efforts are directed to ensuring that for each child leisure reading should be a process of continuous exploration. This seems to be what is meant, in the Library Association's memorandum on the duties of Children's Librarians, by the statement that "once children have been introduced to the library, the Children's Librarian has to encourage them to read *adventurously and wisely*".[1] How sorely in need of guidance some children are will perhaps be illustrated by the following example. A ten-year-old girl brought back to the Library a book by Enid Blyton which she had taken out the previous day and had evidently much enjoyed. Finding no other Blyton on the shelves, and presumably failing to find any other book to suit her tastes, she took out again the very book she had just returned, and on three successive days the self-same thing occurred. A timely suggestion at this point might well have set this child's feet upon new paths of discovery in the world of books ; without such guidance, she and many others like her inevitably confine themselves to the popular favourites tried and recommended by their friends. In watching children in the Public Library, we came to believe that very few of them had much awareness of the range and variety it had to offer. Many appeared to come to the Library with a single author or a single title in mind, and if they found immediately what they were looking for, were satisfied to range no further. If they were unsuccessful at the first attempt, however, they rarely had an alternative in view, or any

---

[1]The Library Association Record, Vol. 62, No. 7. July 1960. pp. 229—230.

way of finding what they wanted other than by examining in turn every book upon the shelves until they came on one to suit their tastes. It so happens in this Library, as in most others, that children's fiction is arranged on the shelves alphabetically by authors, the letter 'A' on shelves nearest the point of entry, the letter 'Z' at the farther end. As a result, a disproportionate number of the books borrowed by our children proved to be by authors whose names begin with letters appearing early in the alphabet, whilst authors not so favoured appear to suffer sad neglect.   This is not intended as advice to would-be authors about their choice of *nom de plume*, but as evidence in support of the contention that children require guidance in their search for books.

Increasingly in recent times, this kind of guidance has come to be regarded as among the most important of the duties of librarians, but clearly no librarian can hope to give personal advice to more than a few of the many children entering his library ; for the rest he can do no more than ensure that on the shelves there are books to suit every reader's tastes and needs, and that his library is so sign-posted and indexed as to enable every child to find his way to what he wants. On the matter of book selection, all that can be said by way of summary is that the first aim must be to find books which will help a child to grow.   Among the 1,500 children's books produced each year, some in any case must inevitably be rejected, and, on the premiss that children look to books to show them how to live, those must surely be rejected which offer them a false image of human life and false notions of the rules and values that apply in it.   We shall not insist on un-relenting realism or factual accuracy, nor do we call for a return to the earnest moralising of the Victorian tale ; there are, however, far too many children's books which skirt carefully round all the facts of life— birth, work, love, marriage, age and death—and which avoid any reference to human feelings other than of fear or courage.   An un-relieved diet of such books cannot ultimately satisfy ; for this a child needs books which illuminate his own experiences.   No book, in short, is good enough for children, which a grown-up cannot read with pleasure and with profit.

On the question of sign-posting and indexing, perhaps, something else remains to be said.   As has been mentioned, it is the common practice in children's libraries to arrange works of fiction on the shelves alphabetically by authors, an arrangement which, however, affords no help to the child who is not familiar with an author or the type of books he writes. Works of non-fiction, on the other hand, are usually disposed upon the shelves in accordance with a classificatory system such as the Dewey Decimal, whereby books which are similar in content are grouped together. Once the reader has the key to this system, he can easily and without assistance find his way to the book he wants, or, in its absence, to another which will do instead. Moreover, the librarian does not need to know every book upon his shelves to be able to find one on a topic in which a reader is interested. In the adult library especially, a system of classification is of the utmost value to the librarian in the task of guiding readers to the works of information that they need, and it is worth considering whether some system of classifying fiction might be of equal value in the children's library.

To be of service to a child, such a system would have to enable him to find with ease the books which meet his needs. A book is likely to be suited to a given reader if its theme is neither too mature nor too childish, but takes him one step forward into life ; if the central character is not too old and not too young, but one with whom the reader may identify himself ; if the book is not too difficult to read and not too easy, but presents him with a satisfying challenge. It seems feasible to devise a system of classifying children's books based on these three facets, and to decide upon a simple code which would summarise this information. A three-letter code might serve the purpose, so that the call-sign ' AAA,' for instance, would indicate a book having as its theme the relationship between child and parent, having a young child as its central character and employing mainly pictures to convey the meaning. Beside it on the shelves might appear a book marked ' AAB ' to show that, though similar to the first in theme and central character, it calls for more effort in the reading, while, further away, another bearing ' BBC ' has a somewhat more mature theme, concerns an older character, and is still more difficult to read.

Two things can be said in favour of a system such as this. The first is that it may simplify for the child the search for books to suit his abilities and needs, and perhaps do something to encourage even the more conservative to attempt a systematic widening of their reading tastes. And secondly, it offers advantages to the librarian. It enables him to see, almost at a glance, the kinds of books his readers chiefly seek, and in what areas the range of choice he offers is inadequate or lacking, thus making it possible for him to judge to what extent his library offers every child the opportunity of a balanced and progressive reading programme.

"The right book to the right child at the right time" is the goal to which our efforts to guide children's reading are directed. The task, in other words, is to put before the child the very book he needs at the moment when he most may profit from it. In order to do this, it is necessary, on the one hand, that we know our reader, his interests and capacities, and the needs he seeks to satisfy through reading, and, on the other, that we know our books, and are able to judge how apt is each to meet a reader's special needs. Because it demands this knowledge, not only of the book but of the reader, individual guidance of this kind falls within the province of the teacher or the school librarian rather than of the librarian at a public library.

An example will perhaps clarify this point and illustrate, too, what is envisaged here by guidance. One ten-year-old girl of high intelligence counts among the books she borrowed in the year such titles as Mabel Esther Allan's *Adventure in Mayo* and *The Amber House,* Irene Byer's *Jewel of the Jungle* and E. H. Porter's *Miss Billy,* all of them clearly indicating the girl's preoccupation with approaching adolescence. At the same time, other books she chooses—Enid Blyton's *Sunny Story Book, Hollow Tree House, The Sea-side Family* and the like—reveal her reluctance to leave the security of childhood. The vacillation evident in her reading, it seems likely, reflects a very real emotional confusion which, if prolonged, could hinder the process of maturing. It might help her to emerge from this confusion to be introduced at this stage to stories—certain of the Careers stories suggest themselves—which show how a new, and no less secure and satisfying, relationship can spring up between the family and the girl who is reaching out towards independence. Only a person who had an insight into her predicament, however, could effect this introduction, and the teacher or the school librarian is clearly better placed than most to do so.

It is recognised, of course, that teachers do not usually regard their responsibility for children's reading in quite this light. While the school has come to accept as one of its main functions to fit the child for healthy personal and social relationships, it has not been the practice, in this country at least, deliberately to exploit recreational reading to this end. The idea is not entirely new, however ; in America, the use of popular children's fiction for rather similar purposes has been strongly advocated in recent times.[1] It has been suggested there, however, that pupils should read privately from a recommended list of children's stories, all having a bearing on some social or emotional problem deemed appropriate to their age, and that thereafter in the classroom pupils should discuss the relevance of the fictional solutions to the problem as it occurs in their own lives. One may readily accept the underlying assumption, that the reading of a story can afford a child new insight into his own difficulties, without, however, subscribing to such a formal and explicit application of the principle as is implied in this procedure. It seems obviously desirable that the books prescribed for study in the class-room should deal with themes which are of real concern to children, and that the moral, social and emotional issues that they raise should be discussed in real, and not merely literary, terms, but the literature lesson is not to be regarded as a fit occasion for group psycho-therapy of any kind, nor, in our view, should a child's private reading be drawn so far into the orbit of formal education. What we envisage is a much more informal and personal approach. A child's leisure reading must remain a private matter, and the rôle of the teacher or the school librarian that of an enthusiastic fellow-reader, with whom it is always easy and pleasant to discuss the books one reads, and who has the happy knack of now and then suggesting a book which proves surprisingly worthwhile. What the child himself may not realise is that the apparently casual suggestion is the outcome of careful study of his previous reading and his present needs.

If it is accepted that this kind of guidance, designed to foster not only reading habits but personal development, is a legitimate responsibility of the teacher, it follows that he should have access to a detailed record of what each child habitually reads. In the primary school, there is much to be said for encouraging each child to keep a journal of his

---

[1]Cf. Heaton and Lewis (1955),

"The technique embodied in this volume grew from the experience of classroom teachers who, knowing the importance of stories and books to children, believed that the printed page could be used to teach attitudes as well as facts—and to teach in the process of entertaining". Foreward, Page v. In the following pages, the authors supply lists of stories suitable for children of a given age, and grouped according to such themes as "Patterns of family life, "How it feels to grow up", "Belonging to groups".

private reading, which he is invited to talk over with the teacher. In the secondary school, it is a fairly easy matter, if a suitable system of issuing books is used, to keep a current record of each pupil's reading from the school library, though it is less possible to know what he reads elsewhere. Records of this kind enable the teacher to reflect upon each pupil's reading experience and to make a number of useful judgements.

He will obviously consider the sheer volume of a pupil's reading, not, of course, in relation to some ideal or average amount, but in the light of what he knows of the child's reading ability and intellectual capacity, and of his other interests and activities. Broadly speaking, he will hope to find a steady growth in the number of books read from year to year as reading skill increases and interest deepens, but he will be as concerned with the child who reads too much, perhaps obsessively as with the one who reads not at all.

Allied to this is another aspect. Ideally, as he grows older and gains fluency in reading, the child should move to books which make more demands upon his powers of understanding. It is not forgotten that the books children read for pleasure are rarely difficult enough to stretch their reading powers, but it is clearly essential, if his interest in books is to outlast childhood, that by the age of eleven or twelve the child should be well accustomed to reading books which in level of difficulty are not far below popular works of adult fiction. Otherwise, when he enters adolescence he will find himself unable to read books on the themes and topics which are relevant to his condition. At the same time, it does not help a child to gain the speed and fluency which are necessary for the enjoyment of reading, to toil laboriously through books beyond his skill, and the teacher will take pains to match the books he recommends to his pupil's known ability.

It is often the child who concentrates entirely on works of information who needs to be persuaded to read easier matter, but for other reasons, too, the teacher will seek to remedy this lack of balance and encourage the reading of a wide variety of books of fiction and non-fiction. The somewhat haphazard reading of works of information on a wide variety of subjects is fairly characteristic of the child of ten or so, and it clearly satisfies a natural and healthy curiosity about the world around. It often accompanies, however, a marked loss of interest in more imaginative writings and even, in some cases, a deep distrust of them, which the teacher will discreetly try to overcome.

Besides attempting to maintain a balance between the amount of fiction and non-fiction read, he will also seek to ensure that the child's reading shows variety, in the sense that the fiction that he reads is not restricted to books of one kind or on a single theme. Boys, with their devouring appetite for Mystery and Adventure stories, are more obviously prone to this kind of conservatism ; superficially, at least, girls appear much more catholic in their tastes. One of the difficulties may be, as has earlier been pointed out, a lack of books—Family stories, Careers stories and Adolescent novels especially—written specifically for boys. Boys and girls alike, however, can be obsessed with books of a certain kind or on a certain theme to the extent of not being able to advance beyond. More often than not, it manifests itself in a reluctance to progress beyond Fantasy or beyond Romance, which the teacher will endeavour to overcome by tactfully suggesting books which treat the same themes in somewhat more realistic terms.

In all this, the teacher's main concern is that his pupil's reading be continuously progressive, that in its difficulty, its themes, and in its degree of realism, it keep pace with, and indeed prepare the way for, the child's advance towards maturity. Much depends upon his having the power to win the pupil's confidence, and an intuitive ability to put himself inside the growing, questing mind, but his insight will be the sharper for some more explicit theory to explain the motives for which children read. To ask of a child's reading to what extent it is symptomatic of a need for emancipation, compensation, recreation or regression will sometimes bring to light its unifying pattern, and so enable the teacher to anticipate, and at need to influence, the way it will unfold.

It must be stressed, of course, that the child's reading is not to be understood or judged *in vacuo*, but must be seen in the context of his whole relationship to his physical surroundings, his family, his friends his work and play, and to himself. It is because a child's personality is so deeply implicated in his reading that there is so much to be gained from knowing what he reads. Were it not so, research into children's reading would have no more point for education than research into the sweets they eat. In a sense, to know what books they like is not what is important ; what matters is that, reading quietly over their shoulder, we should come to know what they are looking for, not in books only, but in life itself. The child intent upon a story has turned his back, however briefly, on all that we, as adults, present to him as real, and, if we heed the criticism thus implied, we shall ask ourselves why what is offered him as education falls so far short of his fiction in giving to him what he manifestly seeks—mystery and adventure, exploration and discovery—and so often fails to enlist his capacities for courage and endurance, generosity and fellow-feeling, loyalty and selflessness. These are the ideals and values which children's books affirm, and they are not by any means contemptible. On the contrary, it is our schools, and our society itself, which stand condemned if it is only through fiction that children can experience them.

LIST OF REFERENCES

BAMBERGER, F. E.
1922

The effects of physical make-up of books upon children's selection.
Baltimore. John Hopkins Press.

BERNSTEIN, Basil
1961

Social class and linguistic development.
Halsey, Floud & Anderson : Education, Economy and Society, pp. 288—314. Glencoe.

BETHNAL GREEN PUBLIC LIBRARIES
1946

Readership Survey.
Bethnal Green.

BOYCE, E. R.
1953

Story books in the Primary school.
Journal of Education, Vol. 85, No. 1011, p. 492.

BREARLEY, M.
1949

An enquiry into the reading tastes and habits of 800 children between seven and eleven years of age.
Unpublished Thesis.
University of Birmingham Library.

BRITISH RESEARCH BUREAU AND MARKET INFORMATION SERVICES
1951

Child Readership Survey.
Hulton Press.

BURT, C.
1959

A Psychological study of typography.
Cambridge University Press.

CAERNARVONSHIRE EDUCATION COMMITTEE
1964

The County Library : Forty-sixth annual report, 1963-64.
Caernarvon.

CARSLEY, J. D.
1957

The interest of children (aged 10—11) in books.
British Journal of Educational Psychology. 27, p. 13.

CENTRAL ADVISORY COUNCIL FOR EDUCATION
1959

15 to 18.
H.M.S.O.

CLARK, Wilson, W.
1958

Boys and Girls : Are there significant ability and achievement differences.
Phi Delta Kappa, XLI, pp. 73—76.

COLEMAN, James S.
1961

Academic achievement and the structure of competition.
Halsey, Floud and Anderson : Education, Economy and Society, pp. 367—387. Glencoe.

CONNOR, D. V.
1954

The relationship between reading achievement and voluntary reading of children.
Educational Review, 6, pp. 221—227.

COSTER, John K.
1958

Attitudes toward school of high school pupils from three income levels.
Journal of Educational Psychology, 49, pp. 61-66.

1959.

Some characteristics of high school pupils from three income groups.
Journal of Education Psychology, 50, pp. 55—65.

DARTON, F. J. H.
1932.

Children's books in England.
Cambridge University Press.

DOUGLAS, J. W. B.
1964

The home and school. A study of ability and attainment in the primary school.
London. McGibbon and Kee.

DOWNING, John A.
1963

Experiments with Pitman's Initial Teaching Alphabet in British schools.
Initial Teaching Alphabet Publications.

DUNLOP, Doris C.
1950

Children's leisure reading interests.
Studies in reading II.
Scottish Council for Research in Education, pp. 81—105.
University of London Press.

ELKIN, Frederick
1950

The psychological aspect of the Hollywood Western.
Journal of Educational Sociology, Vol. 24, No. 2, pp. 72—86.

EYRE, F.
1952

Twentieth century children's books.
London, Longman.

FARR, J. N. and
JENKINS, J. J.
1949

Tables for use with the Flesch readability formula.
Journal of Applied Psychology, 33, pp. 275—278.

FLESCH, R.
1948

A new readability yardstick.
Journal of Applied Psychology, 32, pp. 221—233.

GRIFFITHS, D. C.
1932

The psychology of literary appreciation.
Educational Research Series, No. XIII.
Melbourne University Press.

HAVIGHURST, Robert J.
1961

Education and social mobility in four sociteies.
Halsey, Floud and Anderson : Education,
Economy, and Society, pp. 105—120. Glencoe.

HEATON, Margaret M.,
and LEWIS, Helen B.
1955

Reading ladders for human relationships. Revised
Edition.
American Council on Education.

HOGGART, Richard
1957

The uses of literacy.
Chatto and Windus.

INGLIS, W. B.
1948

The early stages of reading : a review of recent
investigations.
Studies in Reading, I.
Scottish Council for Research in Education.
University of London Press.

JACKSON, B. and
MARSDEN, D.
1962

Education and the working class.
Routledge and Kegan Paul.

JENKINSON, A. J.
1940

What do boys and girls read ?
Methuen.

JONES, W. R.
1955.

Bilingualism and reading ability in English.
University of Wales Press.

JONES, W. R.
MORRISON, J. R.,
ROGERS, J. and SAER, H.
1957

The educational attainment of bilingual children
in relation to their intelligence and linguistic
background.
University of Wales Press.

LADD, Margaret R.
1933

The relation of social, economic and personal
characteristics to reading ability.
Contributions to Education, No. 582.
Bureau of Publications, Teachers' College,
Columbia University.

LAZAR, M.
1937

Reading interests, achievements and opportunities of bright, average and dull children.
Contributions to Education, No. 707.
Bureau of Publications, Teachers' College, University of Columbia.

LEHMAN, H. C. and
WITTY, P. A.
1928.

Sex differences in reference to reading books just for fun.
Education, 48, pp. 602—617.

LESSER, Simon D.
1960

Fiction and the unconscious.
London, Peter Owen.

THE LIBRARY
ASSOCIATION
1960

The duties of children's libraries.
Library Association Record, Vol. 62, No. 7, pp. 229—230.

LIPSCOMB, L. E.
1931

A study of the reading of a sixth grade.
Elementary English Review, 8, pp. 60—63.

LORGE, Irving D.
1944

Predicting Readability.
Teachers' College Record, 45, pp. 404—419.

McCLELLAND, D. C. and
FRIEDMAN, G.A.
1952

A cross-cultural study in the relationship between child-training practices and achievement motivation appearing in folk tales.
Readings in Social Psychology. 2nd Edition, pp. 243—249. New York. Society for the study of Social Issues.

McDONALD, G.
1953

Readability and the popularity of English fiction with secondary modern school pupils.
Unpublished Thesis.
University of Birmingham Library.

McLAREN, Violet M.
1950

Socio-economic status and reading ability : a study in infant reading.
Studies in Reading, II. pp. 2—62. Scottish Council for Research in Education.

MEIGS, Cornelia
1956

A critical history of children's literature.
New York. Macmillan.

MICHAELIS, John U. and
TYLER, Fred T.
1951

A comparison of reading ability and readability.
Journal of Educational Psychology, 42, pp. 491—498.

MITCHELL, Mary A.   The relationship of reading to social acceptability
1949   of sixth grade children.
                       Contributions to Education, No. 953. Bureau of
                          Publications, Teacher's College, Columbia Uni-
                          versity.

MORONEY, M. J.   Facts from figures.
1956   Third Edition. Penguin Books.

MULLETT, M.   A study of the development of reading tastes in
1951   adolescents.
                      Unpublished Thesis. University of Birmingham
                      Library.

PHILPOTT, G. A.   An investigation into motives for reading and their
1953   relation to personal qualities and environmental
                      conditions.
                      Unpublished Thesis. University of Birmingham
                      Library.

SCANLAN, W. J.   One hundred most popular books of children's
1948   fiction selected by children.
                      Elementary English Review, 25, pp. 83—97.

SCHONELL, F. J.   Recent developments in educational research.
1948   British Journal of Educational Psychology, 18,
                      pp. 11—34.

SCOTT, W. J.   Reading, film and radio tastes of high school boys
1947   and girls.
                      New Zealand Council for Educational Research.

SHEFFIELD PUBLIC   Survey of children's reading.
LIBRARIES
1938

SMITH, L. H.   The unreluctant years.
1953   American Library Association.

STOLUROV, L. M. and   A factorial analysis of objective features of printed
NEWMAN, J. R.   language presumably related to reading difficulty.
1959   Journal of Educational Research, Vol. 52, No. 7,
                      pp. 243—251.

SOCIETY OF YOUNG   Survey of London's reading habits.
PUBLISHERS   The Bookseller, January 16th, 1960. pp. 122—
1960   124.

SWARD, B. and
HARRIS, D. B.
1952

The reading ease, human interest value and thematic content of St. Michael's Magazine : a study of children's literature.
Journal of Educational Psychology, 42, pp. 153—165.

TERMAN, Lewis M. and
LIMA, Margaret
1931.

Children's reading.
New York. Appleton,Century.

THORNDIKE, R. L.
1951

Community variables as predictors of intelligence and academic achievement.
Journal of Educational Psychology, 42, pp. 321—338.

TRAXLER, A. E. and
TOWNSEND
1940

Ten years of Research in Reading.
Educational Records Bulletin, No. 32.

TRAXLER, A. E. and
TOWNSEND
1943

Another five years of research in reading.
Educational Records Bulletin. No. 46.

1955

Eight more years of research in reading.
Educational Records Bulletin, No. 64. New York. Educational Records Bureau.

VERNON, M. D.
1960

The investigation of reading problems today.
British Journal of Educational Psychology, 30, pp. 146—154.

WATTS, A. F.
1944

The language and mental development of children.
Harrap.

WESTHILL TRAINING
COLLEGE
1950

80,000 adolescents.
Allen and Unwin.

WHITEHEAD, F.
1956

The attitude of grammar school pupils towards some novels commonly read in school.
British Journal of Educational Psychology, 24, p. 104.

WOLLNER, M. H. B.
1949

Children's voluntary reading as an expression of individuality.
Contributions to Education, No. 944. Bureau of Publications, Teachers' College, Columbia University.

YOUNG, M. and
WILLMOTT, P.
1957

Family and Kinship in East London.
Routledge, Kegan Paul.

ADDITIONAL BIBLIOGRAPHY

Note : Each volume of the *Journal of Educational Research* contains a comprehensive bibliography of studies on reading published in the previous year, compiled by William S. Gray under the title, ' Summary of Reading Investigations.'

AMERICAN LIBRARY
ASSOCIATION
1942

The right book for the right child.
Third edition.
New York : John Day & Co.

AMSDEN, R. H.
1960

Children's preferences in picture story book variables.
Journal of Educational Research, 53, pp. 309—312.

BENE, Eva
1958

Suppression of hetero-sexual interest and of aggression by middle-class and working-class grammar school boys.
British Journal of Educational Psychology, 28, pp. 226—231.

BRAY, D. H.
1962

A study of children's writing on an admired person.
Educational Review. Vol. 15, No. 1, pp. 44—53.

BREW, J. Macalister
1944

Young People and Reading.
Journal of Education, 76, pp. 109—111.

CAPPA, Dan
1950

Types of storybooks enjoyed by kindergarten children.
Journal of Educational Research, Vol. 49, No. 7.

CENTER, S. S. and
PERSONS, G. L.
1936

Leisure reading of New York high school students.
English Journal, 25, pp. 717—726.

CHILD, I. L., POTTER,
E. H., LEVINE, E. M.
1946

Children's text-books and personality development.
Psychological Monographs, Vol. 60, No. 3., pp. 1—54.

COLEMAN, J. H. and
JUNGEBLUT, A.
1961

Children's likes and dislikes about what they read.
Journal of Educational Research, Vol. 54, No. 6, p. 221.

CURR, W., HALLWORTH, H. J., and WILKINSON, 1962
How secondary modern school children spend their time.
Educational Review, Vol. 15, No. 1, pp. 3—9.

DALE, E., and CHALL, J. S. 1948
A formula for predicting readability.
Ohio State University, Educational Research Bulletin, 27, pp. 11—20.

DUNN, F. W. 1921
Interest factors in primary reading material.
Contributions to Education, No. 113. New York.

FOULDS, G. A. 1942
The psychological factors involved in the child's use of fantasy and fiction, and the child's response to fictional characters and its relationship to personality traits. Unpublished thesis.
University of Liverpool.

FRIEDLANDER, K. 1942
Children's books and their function in latency and prepuberty.
American Image, 3.

GOLDHOR, H. 1959
Are the best books the most read ?
Library Quarterly, 29, pp. 251—255.

GUNDERSON, A. C. 1957
What seven-year-olds like in books.
Journal of Educational Research, Vol. 50, No. 7, pp. 509—520.

HAZARD, Paul 1942
Books, Children and Men.
Boston, U.S.A. The Horn Book Co.

JORDAN, A. M. 1926
Children's Interests in reading.
Oxford University Press.

LA BRANT, Lou. L. 1936
An evaluation of free reading in grades ten, eleven and twelve.
Columbus, Ohio. Ohio State University Press.

LEWIS, M. M. 1954 :
Children's reading and illiteracy.
School Librarian, Vol. 7, No. 1. pp. 17—27.

LEYLAND, E. 1937
The Public Library and the Adolescent.
Grafton and Co.

LIBRARY ASSOCIATION 1955
A survey of public library services for children.
London : Library and Information Bureau.

LINES, K. M.
1956

Four to fourteen.
Cambridge University Press.

McLEOD, J.
1962

The estimation of the readability of books of low
difficulty.
British Journal of Educational Psychology, 32,
pp. 112—118.

MILLER, R. A.
1936

The relation of reading characteristics to social
indexes.
American Journal of Sociology, Vol. 41, No. 6.
pp. 738—756.

NORVELL, G. W.
1950

The reading interests of young people.
New York. Heath & Co.

NORVELL, G. W.
1958

What boys and girls like to read.
Morristown, N. J. Silver Burdett Co.

PAFFARD, M. K.
1962

The teaching of English literature in school—a
review of research since 1945.
Educational Review, Vol. IV, No. 3, pp. 218—
229.

PATERSON, D. G. and
TINKER, M.A.

Studies of typographical factors influencing speed
reading.
Journal of Applied Psychology.
Vol. 13, pp. 120—130.
Ibid, pp. 205—219.
Vol. 16, pp. 605—613.

PATERSON, D. G. and
TINKER, M. A.
1940

How to make type readable.
New York. Harper.

POND, F. L.
1952

A simplified method of scoring an inventory of
reading experiences.
Journal of Educational Research, Vol. 45,
No. 8, pp. 585—597.

RANKIN, M.
1944

Children's interests in library books of fiction.
Teachers' College Contributions to Education
No. 906. Columbia University.

RAUSHENBUSCH, E.
1942.

Literature for individual education.
New York. Columbia University Press.

ROBINSON, H. M.
1957

Developing permanent interest in reading.
Cambridge University Press.

ROBINSON, H. M.
1961

Summary of investigations relating to reading.
Journal of Educational Research, Vol. 54, No. 6,
p. 203.

ROSENBLATT, A.
1938

Literature as exploration.
New York. Appleton Century.

SHUTTLEWORTH, F. E.
1932

A critical study of two tests of best books for
children.
Genetic Psychology Monographs, No. 4.

STEWART, M.
1950

The leisure activities of grammar school children.
British Journal of Educational Psychology, 20,
pp. 11—34.

STRANG, Ruth
1942

Exploration in reading patterns.
University of Chicago Press.

STUART, A.
1952

Reading habits in three London boroughs.
Journal of Documentation, Vol. 8, No. 1,
pp. 33—49.

THORNDIKE, R. L.
1941

A comparative study of children's reading interests.
Teachers' College, Columbia University, Bureau of Publications.

TURNER, E. S.
1948

Boys will be boys.
London, Michael Joseph.

VERNON, M. D.
1954

The instruction of children by pictorial illustration.
British Journal of Educational Psychology, 24,
pp. 171—179.

VERNON, P. E.
1950

The estimation of difficulty of vocabulary.
British Journal of Educational Psychology, 20,
pp. 77—82.

WALL, W. D.
1948

The newspaper reading of adolescents and adults.
British Journal of Educational Psychology, 18,
pp. 26—40.

WERTHAM, F.
1955

The seduction of the innocent.
London. Museum Press.

WHITE, Dorothy
1954
Books before five.
Oxford University Press.

WILLIAMS, A. R.
1951
The magazine reading of secondary school children.
British Journal of Educational Psychology, 21, pp. 186—198.

WITTY, F. R.
1955
Children's tastes in book illustration.
The School Librarian. Vol. 7, No. 4, pp. 248—255.

APPENDICES

TABLE I

MEMBERSHIP OF THE LIBRARY

Age	(a) Number in Age group	(b) Number of Readers	(c) Percentage Readers	(d) 95% Confidence Limits
		BOYS		
6 yrs.	72	15	21	± 9.5
7	63	24	38	±12.0
8	70	34	49	±11.7
9	90	48	53	±10.3
10	96	46	48	±10.0
11	89	44	49	±10.3
12	64	28	44	±12.2
All	544	239	44	±4.2
		GIRLS		
6 yrs.	59	24	41	±12.2
7	80	40	50	±11.7
8	57	30	53	±13.0
9	76	38	50	±11.3
10	87	77	89	±6.5
11	73	55	75	±9.9
12	79	52	66	±10.4
All	511	316	62	±4.2
		BOYS AND GIRLS		
6 yrs.	131	39	30	±7.8
7	143	64	45	±8.1
8	127	64	50	±8.7
9	166	86	52	±7.6
10	183	123	67	±6.8
11	162	99	61	±7.5
12	143	80	56	±8.1
All	1,055	555	53	±2.9

Table 2

VOLUME OF BORROWING

Age	Number of Readers	Number of books borrowed	Average per Reader	95% Confidence limits	Standard deviation
yrs.		**Boys**			
6	15	262	17.5	±3.8	14.7
7	24	392	16.3	±2.8	13.5
8	34	552	16.2	±2.5	14.3
9	48	639	13.3	±1.9	12.7
10	46	591	12.8	±1.5	10.1
11	44	893	20.3	±2.7	17.6
12	28	420	15.0	±3.1	17.0
All	239	3,749	15.7	±1.0	15.2
		Girls			
6	24	305	12.7	±2.0	9.9
7	40	517	12.9	±1.8	11.1
8	30	475	15.8	±2.2	11.9
9	38	860	22.6	±3.4	20.6
10	77	2,021	26.2	±2.7	23.5
11	55	1,564	28.4	±2.5	18.7
12	52	1,698	32.6	±4.2	30.6
All	316	7,440	23.5	±1.2	21.4
		Boys and Girls			
6	39	567	14.5	±2.0	12.1
7	64	909	14.5	±1.6	12.5
8	64	1,027	15.7	±1.7	13.4
9	86	1,499	17.4	±1.9	17.3
10	123	2,612	21.2	±1.8	19.8
11	99	2,457	24.8	±2.0	19.4
12	80	2,118	26.5	±2.9	25.7
All	555	11,189	20.2	±.8	19.7

TABLE 3a

Analysis of Issues, showing the number of books in each class as a percentage of the total issues in each age group.

BOYS

Class	6 yrs.	7 yrs.	8 yrs.	9 yrs.	10 yrs.	11 yrs.	12 yrs.
	%	%	%	%	%	%	%
Fantasy							
Puppet	59 ± 5.9	56 ∓ 4.9	28 ± 3.7	6	3	$1 \pm .7$	—
Fairy	17	13	15	9	5	2	3
Animal	3	3	3	3	2	2	2
Juvenile Realism							
School	—	—	—	$1 \pm .8$	$1 \pm .8$	—	$1 \pm .9$
Gang	4	4	8	7	10	12	15
Pony	—	—	1	—	1	—	—
Romance							
Mystery	1 ± 1.2	2 ± 1.4	7	15	20	32	18
Adventure	1	5	17	40 ± 3.8	33 ± 3.7	35 ± 3.1	49 ± 4.7
Adult Realism							
Family	9	10	7	4	3	3	1
Careers	—	—	$1 \pm .8$	—	—	1	—
Adolescent Novel	—	—	—	—	—	—	—
Non-Fiction	6	6	13	15	23	11	10
	100	100	100	100	100	100	100
No. of Books	262	392	552	639	591	893	420

Note : The Confidence Limits given are at the 95% level. In each column, all other limits fall between the two given.

TABLE 3b

Analysis of Issues, showing the number of books in each class as a percentage of the total issues to each age group.

GIRLS

Class	6 yrs.	7 yrs.	8 yrs.	9 yrs.	10 yrs.	11 yrs.	12 yrs.
	%	%	%	%	%	%	%
Fantasy							
Puppet	58 ± 5.5	49 ± 4.9	42 ± 4.5	17	6	3 ± .9	1 ± .4
Fairy	16	18	21	24 ± 2.9	13	9	5
Animal	6	5	5	3	3	4	2
Juvenile Realism							
School	—	—	2	2	8	10	15
Gang	4	5	5	7	9	12	13
Pony	—	1	1 ± .9	3	4	4	6
Romance							
Mystery	1 ± .4	2	7	20	30 ± 2.0	26 ± 2.2	25 ± 2.0
Adventure	—	1 ± .9	2	2	5	7	5
Adult Realism							
Family	11	13	11	14	14	11	10
Careers	—	—	—	—	1 ± .4	4	8
Adolescent Novel	—	—	—	1 ± .6	2	4	7
Non-Fiction	4	7	4	6	5	6	3
	100	100	100	100	100	100	100
No. of Books	305	517	475	860	2,021	1,564	1,698

Note : The Confidence Limits given are at the 95% level. In each column, all other limits fall between the two given.

TABLE 4

Classics among books issued to members of the Library.

Author	Number of Titles	Number of times issued	
		To Boys	To Girls
Alcott, Louisa M.	3	0	11
Andersen, Hans	8	2	21
Austen, Jane	1	0	2
Ballantyne	1	2	1
Blackmore	1	1	0
Barrie, Sir J.	1	0	20
Buchan, J.	3	2	3
Carroll, L.	1	0	6
Conrad, J.	1	1	0
De la Mare, W.	1	0	1
Dickens, C.	5	8	6
Dumas, A.	1	1	0
Eliot, G.	1	0	1
Grahame, K.	3	0	6
Grimm Brothers	5	8	14
Henty, G. A.	2	2	0
Kingsley, C.	1	1	0
Kipling, R.	3	2	4
Lamb, C. and M.	1	2	1
Malory, Sir T.	2	2	5
Marryat, Capt.	1	1	2
Melville, H.	1	5	0
Perrault, C.	1	4	5
Scott, Sir W.	1	1	0
Shakespeare, W.	3	6	2
Stevenson, R. L.	2	10	5
Beecher Stowe, H.	1	1	4
Swift, Dean	1	2	0
Thackeray, W. M.	1	0	2
Twain, Mark	1	5	7
Verne, J.	2	9	6
Wyss, J.	1	0	2
	61	78	139

TABLE 5

Analysis of Non-Fiction issued to Boys and Girls

	Dewey Classification	Issued to Boys		Issued to Girls	
		No.	%	No.	%
000	General Works, Cyclopaedias	13	2.7	8	2.2
100	Philosophy	2	.4	3	.8
200	Religion, Mythology, Bible Stories	17	3.6	50	13.8
300	Sociology	50	10.5	15	4.1
400	Philology	1	.2	2	.6
500	Science	111	23.3	88	24.5
600	Useful Arts	77	16.2	22	6.1
700	Fine Arts, Leisure Pursuits	114	24.0	89	24.5
800	Literature	9	1.7	27	7.5
900	History	19	4.0	14	3.9
	Travel	35	7.7	18	5.0
	Biography	28	5.8	26	7.2
	Total	476	100	362	100

INDEX